Make It Take It

Creating Movement Challenge Kits
for Play at Home or School

Lynn Cox and Terry Lubbers

MAKE IT TAKE IT
Creating Movement Challenge Kits for Play at Home or School

Publisher's Cataloging-in-Publication
(Provided by Quality Books, Inc.)

Cox, Lynn, 1942-
    Make it take it : creating movement challenge
kits for play at home or school / Lynn Cox and
Terry Lubbers.
      p. cm.
      Includes index.
      LCCN: 99-64342
      ISBN: 0-9664413-4-6

      1. Movement education. 2. Teaching—Aids and
devices. 3. Physical education for children.
4. Early childhood education—Activity programs.
I. Lubbers, Terry. II. Title.

GV452.C69 2000   372.86'044
                        QBI99-1041

Published by **TEKNA BOOKS**™
www.teknabooks.com

Printed in the USA by Morris Publishing
3212 East Hwy 30, Kearney, NE 68847
1-800-650-7888

        1   2   3   4   5   99 00 01 02 03

Children have real understanding only of that
which they invent themselves, and each time
that we try to teach them something too quickly, we
keep them from reinventing it themselves.

Jean Piaget

Table of Contents

ACKNOWLEDGEMENTS

We are greatly appreciative to the many persons who made this book a reality. This includes preschool, kindergarten, and elementary teachers, and adapted physical educators who encouraged us to put the movement challenges into a user-friendly format, colleagues who were willing to read through the text and provide helpful suggestions, parents and families who have field tested the movement challenges in their homes, and the enthusiastic, creative children who could always find "one more way" to do an activity.

Special thanks to Kris and Rebecca Cox of Tekna Books; support from Jerry Cox; Lee Coleman, who planted a seed for lifelong learning and teaching; Cindy Gallagher for the group silhouette idea; illustrator Howard Hanson; text readers Adele Bauer, Robin Henslin, Kim Riesgraf, and Stef Rodesch; consultation from Dr. Allen Burton; and of course the kids: David Eli, Kelsi Jo, Michael, Bryanne, Ahmed, Aubrey, Kamesha, Kunal, Travis, Brett, and many more . . .

ABOUT THE AUTHORS

Lynn Cox and Terry Lubbers have over 45 years of combined experience teaching physical education and developmental/adapted physical education in public schools. Their work has focused on young children, both typically developing and with special needs. Lynn and Terry have been instrumental in providing movement experiences for families at home and in the community. They have been invited to serve on state and school district writing teams as well as being in demand for presentations in college classes, workshops, and conferences.

Part 1
INTRODUCTION TO KIT MAKING

WHY USE THE KITS?

The concepts and principles of motor development demonstrate the need for young children to have the opportunity for exposure to a wide variety of movement experiences and to practice movement tasks through play for successful development of skills. As children are learning to move, they are moving to learn and developing as a whole child—physically, mentally, and socially.

Direct educational services by professionals trained in motor development for young children are often limited. Thus, parents and primary caregivers who are the "first teachers" of young children are often the source for providing experiences and the environment for learning. The need expressed by these **parents and day care providers**, as well as by **leaders of community recreation programs**, **preschool teachers**, **primary-grade elementary teachers**, **physical educators**, **developmental/adapted physical education teachers and therapists** to have a source of quick/easy directions and materials for an array of developmentally appropriate gross motor movement challenges that are child sensitive and user friendly are the basis for this book. The movement challenges, which incorporate a piece of equipment, are designed to facilitate the many facets of a child's development.

The selected ten topics/pieces of equipment in this book are hopefully a springboard to awareness, creativity, and discovery of many other movement challenges. Use of different, simple equipment by educators, recreation leaders, and caregivers/parents will increase children's exposure and participation in the joy of learning through moving.

WHO USES THE KITS?

Parents/Caregivers:

Construction of movement challenge kits that are inexpensive to create, that are attractive/motivating in design, easily portable, and include a variety of movement challenges might be one use of the materials included in this book. Parents might wish to create kits for everyday play at home with their children. The kits could be available for spontaneous play inside or outside, or as a "take-along" activity when going to a different place (vacation, visit grandparents etc.).

Frequently parents ask the professional educator, "How can I play with my child at home to improve motor development?" Thus, the movement challenge kit may be a parent education tool for the professionally trained motor educator or therapist to provide activity ideas and information for stimulating creative play as well as information for safety, reinforcement, and feedback to the child. Through play with carefully designed activities, the parent/caregiver may also gain awareness of the child's strengths and needs, learning styles, and length of attention span. This information may be helpful for sharing in the home-school partnership of learning. Use of a movement challenge kit would hopefully stimulate other ways to create spontaneous motor play (i.e. what are other different ways you could...). Parents/caregivers, as teachers, are thus actively involved in expanding learning experiences for their children.

The professional movement specialist might solicit parent involvement in ways such as: formal or informal parent conferences, questionnaires, presentations with students or program/school newsletters. A check-out system similar to a book or toy lending library, may be helpful. A maximum time for keeping a kit, a limit of number of kits at a time, and other logistics may need planning for success. (See Appendix for sample check-out forms.)

Teacher/Community Recreation Leaders:

Teachers/recreation leaders of young children in primary grades, preschools, and day care homes or centers may want to select certain activities for use in their daily plans that they prepare for children individually, in groups, or in learning centers. Children with special needs are frequently included in early childhood settings and also benefit from activities that fit their development and abilities. The variety of activity options allows the teacher/leader to provide for different rates of development of all children rather than to just teach an activity. Adaptations, if needed, can be made to ensure all an opportunity to participate.

School or community environments that have limited space may find success with selection of a few movement challenges from one activity kit to be used in a movement play station. Periodically the movement challenges can be changed to meet new developing abilities and interests. Because the activities are not locked into a formal lesson plan, the educator/leader can build on what children know and can do for the discovery and learning of new skills and understanding. (See Appendix for example of a play station format).

Special Educator/Therapists:

Educators of children with special needs, especially developmental/adapted physical educators and therapists, may wish to use movement challenge kits at home or at school as a regular part of programming for children that they serve. Movement challenge kits can provide additional guided practice and reinforcement for development of motor abilities.

HOW TO MAKE A KIT

Assembling a movement challenge kit is as easy as "1-2-3"

1. Obtain or create a container/packaging

2. Make or buy the equipment

3. Add a packet of movement challenge instructions

At the beginning of each section there is a page outlining some suggestions on what to include in each movement challenge kit. However, kits may be constructed in varying ways to fit individual or program needs.

1. Container

A variety of containers or packaging can be used. Ziplock™-type bags are inexpensive, lightweight, and readily available. Small boxes that may be available from sources such as school food service or department stores are another option. Cloth bags may be sewn by volunteer parents or as a project or extra credit option in a sewing class within the school system.

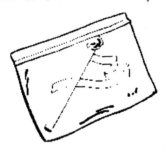
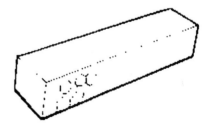

2. Equipment

All of the equipment needed to participate in the movement challenges is commercially available. However, most of the primary or supplemental equipment can be made and construction directions are included for these items. It is recommended that equipment be lightweight and easily portable. Because children may not remember to return kits and/or parts from kits get lost or are expendable, it is suggested that the cost of replacing each kit be kept relatively low. Equipment that is easily sanitized between uses or that doesn't need to be returned may be preferred.

Place the equipment in the activity kit container.

3. Instructions and Movement Challenges Packet

<u>The instruction and movement challenge kit pages and appendix material from this book may be reproduced.</u> The number of pages, level of difficulty, along with selected instructional pages, (i.e. what children will gain, safety, how you can help.....) may be selected for an individual kit.

The flexibility of selecting specific movement challenges allows professional educators to use their expertise to include developmentally appropriate tasks from the options to meet the child's critical points in maturation when motor skills are most effectively learned. Movement challenges can be copied onto different colored sheets of paper for ease and speed of identification. They are found in a general developmental order with tasks appropriate for preschool children occurring before tasks for kindergarten and early elementary.

Instruction pages/movement challenge sheets can be laminated to provide a more durable copy. However, non-laminated copies of instructions may be preferred for teacher-added comments or deletions. Some parents and professionals may wish to keep the copy of the selected activities for future reference.

Whether kits are used at home or in other educational settings, it is suggested that only a few movement challenge pages be included in a kit at a time. Children's attention spans may be short and parents/caregivers may feel overwhelmed if there is too much for them to do. The purpose of the kits is to provide enjoyable activities for everyday play, not a laundry list of what must be done.

Many of the movement challenges can be enhanced with the use of music to help the child's motivation and organization of play. For example, a favorite piece of music could be used to organize a child's play/practice time. ("Can you keep trying to...until the music stops?")

Place the instruction and movement challenge pages in the kit container.

Part 2

MOVEMENT CHALLENGE KITS

CREATING MOVEMENT WITH BALLOONS AND BALLOON BALLS

A Collection of Movement Challenges

Balloons are very portable. Before inflation, they can be tucked into a pocket, purse, or backpack and are available for play at a moment's notice.

The balloon ball, a balloon with a fabric cover, likewise offers an easily stored and carried play item. With simple modifications, it offers a variety of activities similar to and yet different from balloon play.

Kit Contents

1. Container

Ziplock™-type bag, cloth bag, or box

2. Equipment

Balloons—recommend standard round size in an assortment of colors. Allow plenty for breakage and doubling. Doubling is one balloon rolled up and inserted inside another balloon. Necks of both balloons should be kept together when filling with air. With necks of both balloons held together, tie them off as a unit. Double balloons are heavier and have a faster flight.

Fabric balloon ball cover(s). A commercial variety of a balloon ball is called a Balzac™.

3. Instructions and Movement Challenge Packet

Decorative "cover page" (may wish to laminate)

Instructional pages that explain what children will gain, safety precautions, and hints on how you can help

Movement challenge pages

Instructions for inflating a balloon ball and variations

Balloon Ball Construction

1. Select fabric. Light colored plain fabric could be chosen and decorated with permanent markers. Children might want to do this to personalize their ball. Or, use bright colored fabric or combinations of bright colored fabric for different panels to make these balloon coverings attractive.

2. Cut out six same-sized cloth panels of a narrow barrel shape (see diagram). These are the side panels. A panel from an old beach ball could be used as a pattern.

3. Cut out two (a top and a bottom) hexagon-shaped pieces of fabric. The length of one of its sides is the same length as the end of the barrel-shaped panel.

4. Make an opening (button hole or a slit lined with Velcro™) in the middle of one of the hexagon-shaped pieces.

5. Sew the sides of the barrel-shaped panels together and then sew their ends to the hexagon-shaped end panels.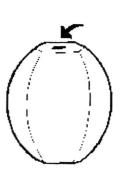

Balloon Ball Inflation

1. Put balloon into fabric cover through hole in hexagon-shaped piece. The mouthpiece of balloon should stick out through the hole.

2. Fill the balloon with air while it is inside cover until it fits tightly.

3.   Tie off balloon near the mouthpiece and push the blowing piece/stub inside the cover.

4.   To deflate the balloon ball, puncture the balloon and take it out of the cloth cover for disposal.

Balloon Ball Variations

1.   Put **rice, popcorn kernels, dried split peas, or lentils** in the balloon before inflating. Children will enjoy the sounds as the balloon ball is used.

2.   Put **coins or other flat weighted materials** in the fabric cover before you blow up the balloon. When the balloon is blown up, it will hold the weights in place.   The weights will make the balloon ball move off balance for a greater challenge.

3.   Put **water** in the balloon before inflating. Try using different amounts of water. It is best to use the water-filled balloon ball outside. This type of balloon ball may be fun to play with in a pool or at a beach.

CREATING MOVEMENT WITH BALLOONS AND BALLOON BALLS

A Collection of Movement Challenges

Balloons are very portable. Before inflation, they can be tucked into a pocket, purse, or backpack and are available for play at a moment's notice.

The balloon ball, a balloon with a fabric cover, likewise offers an easily stored and carried play item. With simple modifications, it offers a variety of activities similar to and yet different from balloon play.

INSTRUCTION AND MOVEMENT CHALLENGE PACKET
"Make It Take It" ISBN 0-9664413-4-6   Copyright 1999, L. Cox and T. Lubbers

Balloons and Balloon Balls: Instructions

What children will gain:

- eye-hand coordination
- eye-foot coordination
- balance
- bilateral coordination
- visual tracking

- body/space awareness
- body control
- physical fitness
- sequencing

Through play, the development of motor patterns will assist in building motor skills for use in lifelong enjoyment of movement activities. Because balloons and balloon balls move through the air and are "soft" when touching the body, children are often willing to attempt more difficult activities without fear of getting hurt.

Safety:

✓ Adults should inflate and *closely supervise young children's use of balloons.* Young children could suffocate by an uninflated balloon or choke on a piece of broken balloon. Do not allow children to put balloons or broken pieces of balloons in their mouth.

✓ Balloons should be inflated only moderately because high inflation increases the chance of breakage.

✓ Children may need assistance in determining a safe amount of space needed for a particular activity.

✓ Emphasize moving and directing the balloon or balloon ball into "empty" spaces to avoid collisions with objects or persons.

✓ If balloon balls are used at a pool or beach *never consider/use it as a means of flotation.*

INSTRUCTION AND MOVEMENT CHALLENGE PACKET
"Make It Take It" ISBN 0-9664413-4-6   © 1999, L. Cox and T. Lubbers
This page is reproducible

How you can help:

✓ Encourage eye contact with the balloon or balloon ball.

✓ Encourage thinking of different ways to accomplish the suggested activities.

INSTRUCTION AND MOVEMENT CHALLENGE PACKET
"Make It Take It" ISBN 0-9664413-4-6   © 1999, L. Cox and T. Lubbers
This page is reproducible

Balloon Inflation

1. <u>Single Balloon</u>.   Inflate moderately.   High inflation increases breakage.

2. <u>Double Balloon</u>. Roll-up one balloon and insert inside the second balloon. Keep necks of both balloons together when filling with air. Tie them off as a unit.

Balloon Ball Inflation

1. Put balloon into fabric cover through hole in hexagon-shaped piece. The mouthpiece of balloon should stick out through the hole.

2. Fill the balloon with air while it is inside cover until it fits tightly.

3. Tie off balloon near the mouthpiece and push the blowing piece/stub inside the cover.

4. To deflate the balloon ball, puncture the balloon and take it out of the cloth cover for disposal.

Balloon Ball Use Variations

1. Put some **rice, popcorn kernels, dried split peas, or lentils** in the balloon before inflating. Children will enjoy the sounds as the balloon ball is used.

2. Put some **coins or other flat weighted materials** in the fabric cover before you blow up the balloon. When the balloon is blown up, it will hold the weights in place. The weights will make the balloon ball move off balance for a greater challenge.

INSTRUCTION AND MOVEMENT CHALLENGE PACKET
"Make It Take It" ISBN 0-9664413-4-6   © 1999, L. Cox and T. Lubbers

3. Put some **water** in the balloon before inflating. Try using different amounts of water. It is best to use the water-filled balloon ball outside. This type of balloon ball may be fun to play with in a pool or beach.

INSTRUCTION AND MOVEMENT CHALLENGE PACKET
"Make It Take It" ISBN 0-9664413-4-6   © 1999, L. Cox and T. Lubbers

Balloons and Balloon Balls: Movement Challenges

With a balloon or balloon ball can you...

✓ put it on your knee, foot, back, head, or on other body parts?

✓ move it between your legs, over your shoulder, under your foot, and around you waist/tummy?

✓ jump up and touch it if someone holds it a little higher than you can reach?

✓ catch it when tossed to you?

✓ toss it up and catch it?

Can you tap or hit the balloon or balloon ball...

✓ when it is suspended from a string or rope from a door frame or a tree branch?

- with different body parts?
- with a foot or both feet when laying down?
- by kicking it with one foot while you are standing? How many times can you kick it in a row?

✓ while in different positions such as kneeling or sitting?

✓ in the air once? How many times can you tap or hit the balloon or balloon ball before it touches the floor?

✓ with gentle taps? With strong/forceful taps?

✓ alternating left and right hands?

INSTRUCTION AND MOVEMENT CHALLENGE PACKET
"Make It Take It" ISBN 0-9664413-4-6   © 1999, L. Cox and T. Lubbers

With a balloon or balloon ball can you...

✓ kick it? Try kicking it with the side of your foot or your toe. Can you dribble it like a soccer ball?

✓ throw it and hit an empty milk carton placed on the floor? Can you knock the milk carton over?

✓ hit or tap it in the air using a cardboard tube from a paper towel roll, a paper plate, or a wooden spoon?

   - how many times in a row can you do this?
   - hit it along the floor from one location to another?

With a friend can you...

✓ roll a balloon ball on the floor to each other? Can you use different body parts such as head, elbow, or toes to roll it to each other?

✓ pass a balloon or balloon ball between your legs like hiking a football?

✓ play catch with a balloon or balloon ball?

✓ tap a balloon or balloon ball back and forth to each other? Play "keep it up" by seeing how many successive taps you can make to each other before the balloon or balloon ball hits the floor.

✓ kick a balloon or balloon ball back and forth?

With a balloon or balloon ball can you...

✓ walk across the room hitting it as you walk?

INSTRUCTION AND MOVEMENT CHALLENGE PACKET
"Make It Take It" ISBN 0-9664413-4-6   © 1999, L. Cox and T. Lubbers
This page is reproducible

- walk in different directions such as forward, backward, or sideways?
- walk in different patterns such as in a circle or zig-zag?

✓ throw it in the air, touch your hips (or other body part), and then catch it?

✓ place the balloon or balloon ball between your knees and jump across the room without letting it fall to the floor?

✓ drop it and kick it while standing? While sitting on a bench or chair?

✓ tap it in the air, turn in a circle, and catch the balloon?

With a friend, can you...

✓ hit the balloon or balloon ball back and forth over a net? How many times can you hit it across the net before it touches the floor?

- hit the balloon or balloon ball over the net while in different positions such as sitting or kneeling?
- hit the balloon or balloon ball over the net by striking it with a wooden spoon, a cardboard tube from paper towels, or a sturdy paper plate?

To make a net, tie a string or rope between two chairs. If desired, tape or drape sheets or strips of newspaper from the string to make a solid-looking net.

INSTRUCTION AND MOVEMENT CHALLENGE PACKET
"Make It Take It" ISBN 0-9664413-4-6 © 1999, L. Cox and T. Lubbers
This page is reproducible

With a friend can you...

✓ sit facing each other and pass the balloon or balloon ball from feet to feet with out letting it drop?

✓ lay on your back with your feet next to your friend and pass the balloon or balloon ball from feet to feet?

✓ place the balloon or balloon ball between your left hip and your friend's right hip and walk across the room without using your hands to hold it in place? Use other body parts such as elbows, knees, back, or stomach to hold the balloon or balloon ball in place while moving across the room.

✓ hit the balloon or balloon ball back and forth as you walk across the room?

✓ tap a balloon or balloon ball back and forth to each other using different body parts such as thumb, elbow, knee, or head?

Can you hit the balloon or balloon ball in the air and...

✓ clap your hands and catch it?

✓ touch the floor and catch it after it bounces? (With a balloon ball you may be able to catch it after it bounces.)

✓ tap it with a sequence of body parts such as knee, then shoulder, then knee, then shoulder? If this is difficult, alternate hitting the balloon with your hand and another body part. An example of this sequence is tapping the balloon or balloon ball with hand, then knee, then hand.

INSTRUCTION AND MOVEMENT CHALLENGE PACKET
"Make It Take It" ISBN 0-9664413-4-6   © 1999, L. Cox and T. Lubbers

With a balloon or balloon ball can you...

✓ hit it in the air as many times as possible while keeping one foot on a flattened grocery bag, carpet square or other object? (Restricting movement by keeping one foot in place requires greater eye-hand control.)

✓ drop it, let it bounce, and then catch it?

✓ place it on the floor and make it move across the floor by throwing or rolling crunched up newspaper balls at it?

✓ keep it up in the air by tapping it with a wooden spoon or cardboard tube from paper towels while walking on your knees?

✓ keep hitting it while you change positions from standing to sitting? From kneeling to lying on your back? From standing to lying on your side?

✓ tap it in the air with different body parts such as finger, foot, or fist while lying on your back?

✓ strike it with a cardboard paper towel tube: first with the end of the tube and then with the length of the tube?

✓ tap it in the air using five or more different body parts within a 30 second time period without letting the balloon or balloon ball touch the floor?

With a friend can you...

✓ join hands to form a small circle and try to keep the balloon or balloon ball in the air by hitting it with your joined hands? Working together, how many times can both of you tap the balloon or balloon

INSTRUCTION AND MOVEMENT CHALLENGE PACKET
"Make It Take It" ISBN 0-9664413-4-6   © 1999, L. Cox and T. Lubbers
This page is reproducible

ball in the air before it touches the floor? Join hands with several friends to form a larger circle and try this activity.

✓ hold a towel or small blanket by the corners, place the balloon or balloon ball in the middle of the towel, lift the towel to toss it in the air, and catch it on the towel? How many times can you do this in a row without it hitting the floor?

INSTRUCTION AND MOVEMENT CHALLENGE PACKET
"Make It Take It" ISBN 0-9664413-4-6   © 1999, L. Cox and T. Lubbers
This page is reproducible

CREATING MOVEMENT WITH BALLS

A Collection of Movement Challenges

Children and balls have long been catalysts for many hours of play alone or with others. Balls come in many shapes and sizes. This makes play with balls full of potential for children's motor development especially eye-hand coordination. Activities with balls may be exploratory in nature or may be more specifically focused for learning the fundamental motor skills of receipt and propulsion of objects (catching and throwing). This leads to participation and skills used in low organized games and sports.

Kit Contents

1. Container

Ziplock™-type bag, cloth or box

2. Equipment

The size, shape, and make-up of a ball may determine how it is used. A ball that is small enough to hold in a hand may be caught and is thrown differently than one that is larger. The density of a ball is important to consider. A lightweight foam/Nerf™ material vs. a heavier rubber ball may be less threatening to a child learning to catch.

Balls can be obtained at a variety of local stores or from sports equipment catalogues. Generically balls are known by activity use such as table tennis balls, golf balls, tennis balls, baseballs, beach balls, soccer balls, footballs, basketballs, or playground balls. Examples of "trade name" balls would include Koosh™, Gertie™, Geodesic™, PocoBall™, Slo-mo™, Squellet™, Globalls™, Bumpballs™, and Spider Balls™. Balls can also be made from common/everyday materials. See directions for three types of balls (yarn, stocking, and paper balls).

3. Instructions and Movement Challenge Packet

Decorative "cover page" (may wish to laminate)

Instructional pages that explain what children will gain, safety precautions, and hints on how you can help.

Movement challenge pages

HOMEMADE BALL IDEAS

Yarn Ball Construction

Materials: Knitting yarn of varied colors and thickness, two cardboard circles (diameter could vary - suggested is 4"-6"), and nylon or cotton string.

Construction:

1.   Cut a round hole about one inch in diameter in the center of two cardboard circle. This makes the cardboard look like a donut.

3.   Put cardboard pieces together. Cut about 3-4 yards of yarn and wrap yarn around cardboard donut from center out.   Continue wrapping other pieces of yarn around the cardboard until desired thickness.

3.   With a scissors, cut the yarn between the outside edges of the cardboard.

4.   Wrap string between the cardboard and tie tightly. Do this twice. Remove cardboard.

5.   Fluff the yarn into a ball and trim any long pieces.

Stocking Ball Construction

Materials: Nylon stocking and stuffing (rags, fiber fill, pieces of old nylon stockings).

Construction:

1. Stuff the toe of the stocking with pieces of rags, fiber fill or other old nylon stockings.

2. Tie a knot in the stocking.

3. Clip off remaining end.

Newspaper Ball Construction

Materials: Newspaper, 7-9 strips of cloth, approximately 1"-2" in width, and vinyl tape (colored tape optional).

Construction:

1. Crumple and wad several sheets of newspaper (amount determines size of ball).

2. Wrap with cloth strips and pull tightly while maintaining the round shape.

3. To hold strips in place, cover with a layer of tape. Or, crumple newspaper and wrap with masking tape into ball shape.

CREATING MOVEMENT WITH BALLS

A Collection of Movement Challenges

Children and balls have long been catalysts for many hours of play alone or with others. Balls come in many shapes and sizes. This makes play with balls full of potential for children's motor development especially eye-hand coordination. Activities with balls may be exploratory in nature or may be more specifically focused for learning the fundamental motor skills of receipt and propulsion of objects (catching and throwing). This leads to participation and skills used in low organized games and sports.

INSTRUCTION AND MOVEMENT CHALLENGE PACKET
"Make It Take It" ISBN 0-9664413-4-6   Copyright 1999, L. Cox and T. Lubbers

Balls: Instructions

What children will gain:

- ✿ eye-hand coordination
- ✿ eye-foot coordination
- ✿ body/space awareness
- ✿ sequencing skills

- ✿ body control
- ✿ physical fitness
- ✿ bilateral coordination
- ✿ visual tracking

Balls provide a media for children to explore movement and develop fundamental motor skills that will allow them to enjoy activities individually and with friends. Beginning activities lead to skills that are foundational for participation in low organized games and sports.

Safety:

- ✓ Allow sufficient space so that balls that are kicked or thrown will not hit breakable objects or rebound in an unsafe way.

- ✓ Balls should be provided that accommodate the developmental skill level of the child i.e. softer balls (Nerf™, yarn) for the less skilled child vs. higher density balls (rubber playground ball, soccer ball) for the higher skilled child.

How you can help:

- ✓ Encourage child to keep eyes on/watch the ball.

- ✓ Practice the motions of throwing and catching without the ball before using the ball.

- ✓ When a ball is being tossed/thrown for catching, begin with shorter distances and increase the distance as skills develop.

40

"Make It Take It" ISBN 0-9664413-4-6   © 1999, L. Cox and T. Lubbers

✓ When a child is beginning to develop catching skills, try to toss the ball to him/her in a slow-moving arc that lands at about chest height. As catching skills increase, throw the ball to the right, left, high, low to increase the challenge.

✓ Use cue words. For overhand throwing --- "hand by ear". For catching --- "hands ready".

✓ For beginners, suggest pointing your hand at the target when ball is released.

INSTRUCTION AND MOVEMENT CHALLENGE PACKET
"Make It Take It" ISBN 0-9664413-4-6   © 1999, L. Cox and T. Lubbers
This page is reproducible

Ball Movement Challenges

Can you...

- ✓ put the ball on different body parts (i.e. on your head, on your knee, on your foot, on your front/back/side)?

- ✓ hold the ball high, low, between your legs, or under your foot?

- ✓ stand holding the ball above your head, slowly sit down while keeping the ball above your head?

- ✓ hold the ball in different ways (i.e. between your knees, between your elbows, between your wrists, between your feet while sitting down, in your right hand while you balance on your right or left foot)?

- ✓ sit and move/roll the ball on the ground around your body, under your knees (let them be a tunnel)?

- ✓ move, roll, bounce, or throw the ball using only one hand? What else can you do with the ball using only one hand?

- ✓ move the ball around your body waist high, neck high, knee high, or between your legs in a figure eight pattern?

- ✓ roll the ball on the floor while on hands and knees, guiding it with your forehead?

- ✓ place the ball on the ground and jump around it, hop or gallop around it?

- ✓ place the ball on the floor and go over the ball without touching it? Try going over it a different way. Jump forward over your ball? Jump backward or sideways? Try jumping over it three times.

42

"Make It Take It" ISBN 0-9664413-4-6   © 1999, L. Cox and T. Lubbers

✓ hold the ball between your knees and jump like a kangaroo?

✓ jump over the ball that a friend has rolled toward you?

✓ put the ball on a non-carpeted surface, place your fingers on the ball and spin it like a top?

Can you roll the ball...

✓ back and forth to a friend? Use two hands or one hand.

✓ under a table, chair, or between a friend's legs (who makes a tunnel by standing with their feet apart)?

✓ and knock over paper milk carton containers/plastic two-liter pop bottles (or other bowling-type targets)? Increase the distance for greater challenge.

✓ against a wall and catch it after it rebounds off the wall?

✓ and then run and catch up with it/pick it up while it is rolling?

✓ and run around it while it is rolling?

Can you...

✓ throw the ball into an empty pail or clothes basket?

✓ catch a ball that someone throws to you?

✓ throw the ball high and still catch it? How did you make it go higher?

INSTRUCTION AND MOVEMENT CHALLENGE PACKET
"Make It Take It" ISBN 0-9664413-4-6   © 1999, L. Cox and T. Lubbers

✓ toss the ball in front of you, run forward, and catch it?   Or, toss it near your side and try to catch it?

✓ toss the ball with your right hand and catch it with your left - or left to right?

✓ toss the ball in the air, clap your hands and catch the ball?

✓ toss the ball in the air, touch your knees and catch the ball? Can you throw it in the air and touch two different body parts, and then catch the ball?

✓ toss the ball up and catch it while walking, running, galloping, or skipping?

✓ toss the ball in the air, sit down and catch it? Toss ball up, stand up and catch it.

✓ toss the ball to a wall, let it bounce once, then catch it?

Can you...

✓ drop the ball and catch it after it bounces? Hold the ball over your head or below your knees, drop it and catch it.

✓ bounce the ball, clap your hands, and then catch the ball? Try while sitting or kneeling.

✓ bounce the ball under your right leg and catch it?

✓ hold the ball in your right hand, drop it and catch it with your left hand?

✓ hold the ball behind your head, drop it, turn around, and catch it?

INSTRUCTION AND MOVEMENT CHALLENGE PACKET
"Make It Take It" ISBN 0-9664413-4-6   © 1999, L. Cox and T. Lubbers
This page is reproducible

✓ drop and catch the ball while walking?

Can you kick a ball...

✓ while standing? (the ball is stationary)

✓ using light or strong kicks?

✓ using different parts of your foot, i.e. toe, heel, side?

✓ a short distance? A far distance?

✓ at a target?

✓ that is rolled to you? i.e. standing or running toward it

✓ so that it goes high in the air?

✓ using little taps and moving with it?

With a friend, can you...

✓ kick a ball back and forth to each other?

✓ stop a ball without using your hands that is kicked or rolled to you?

✓ kick the ball to each other while moving?

INSTRUCTION AND MOVEMENT CHALLENGE PACKET
"Make It Take It" ISBN 0-9664413-4-6   © 1999, L. Cox and T. Lubbers

With friend(s) can you...

Play the game, **HOT POTATO**: While music is playing, sit or stand in a circle with a group of friends and pass or toss the ball around the circle until a sound cue is given (whistle blow, drum beats, music stops etc.). At the signal, participants playing the game pass or toss the ball in the opposite direction. Different kinds of passes could be tried such as underhand throw, overhand throw, or moving the ball between your legs.

Play the game, **MOVE BACK**: Toss and catch the ball with a friend. If a person misses he/she takes a step forward, if he/she catches the ball move back a step.

Play the game, **SEVEN-UP**: Toss the ball to a wall. Let it bounce once then catch it while saying "one up". Repeat six more times each time saying, "two up, or three up . . . seven up." Next add a new challenge (i.e. clap hands or turn around in a circle before catching the ball) while repeating the "one up, two up,...,seven up" count. Continue with a new challenge until seven different challenges are completed. The game may be played alternating turns with friend(s) for each new challenge.

Play **KEEP AWAY/PICKLE IN THE MIDDLE**: Two players throw and catch a ball with each other while a third person who is between them tries to intercept/catch the ball. If the middle person succeeds in intercepting the ball, the person who threw it becomes the middle player. After a set number of tosses (i.e. ten), if the same person is still in the middle, rotate one of the tossing/catching players into the middle.

INSTRUCTION AND MOVEMENT CHALLENGE PACKET
"Make It Take It" ISBN 0-9664413-4-6   © 1999, L. Cox and T. Lubbers
This page is reproducible

Throwing Balls

Development of the Overhand Throwing

Children's overhand throwing skills begin when a child holds the ball in two hands and pushes it away from his/her chest. This is followed by holding the ball in one hand and slinging it across the body, releasing it in a sideways direction. Next, the child stands with feet stationary (positioned side by side), brings the ball above the shoulder near the ear, and propels it forward in a "chop" motion (forearm only going forward).

The throwing pattern moves toward maturity as the child throws the ball with hand passing above the shoulder following through across the body after the ball is released (incorporating trunk rotation) while stepping forward with one foot. Developmentally, the child will step forward with the foot on the same side as the throwing arm before advancing to the stage of stepping forward with the opposite foot.

Development of the Underhand Throwing

Children's underhand throwing skills begin when a child stands with feet together (side by side), swings the throwing arm from back to front below the waist, and releases the ball in front of the body in desired direction. However, timing of the release in a beginning throw/toss may be difficult and may be done too soon or too late causing the ball to be propelled in an unintended direction.

Next in developmental progression, the child will step forward on the same side as the throwing arm with arm back-swing often occurring before the leg movement.

The more mature pattern occurs when the child steps forward with the foot that is opposite the throwing arm. The length of stride increases, and weight is shifted from the back to forward foot during release of the ball. At this stage, the throwing arm rhythmically swings in a downward and

INSTRUCTION AND MOVEMENT CHALLENGE PACKET
"Make It Take It" ISBN 0-9664413-4-6   © 1999, L. Cox and T. Lubbers

backward arc before swinging forward with release of ball in intended direction (arm following through in arc pathway).

Ways to Practice Throwing

1.   Practice in the more stable position of sitting before upright/standing.

2.   Practice with hand-over-hand assistance of adult (holding/touching/maneuvering the child's arm and hand above the shoulder for an overhand throw.)

3.   Have the child watch someone throw the ball.

4.   Practice the motion of throwing without the ball. Break the action into smaller parts (i.e. the forward step, the arm motion) before combining.

5.   Draw or tape tagboard (or other material) footprints on the floor for the child to match his/her feet for incorporating the forward step.

6.   Try different sizes of balls. Studies have shown that ball size may dictate how a ball is propelled.

Helpful Hints

Use word cues:
-    Overhand: "put hand up by your ear", "move arm back", "step while throwing"
-    Underhand: "swing arm like a swing/pendulum," "reach with your hand (on the forward swing) where you want the ball to go."

INSTRUCTION AND MOVEMENT CHALLENGE PACKET
"Make It Take It" ISBN 0-9664413-4-6   © 1999, L. Cox and T. Lubbers
This page is reproducible

Catching Balls

Development of Catching

Children's catching skills evolve in a developmental progression. Initially, the child receives or catches a ball as it rebounds off his/her chest and traps it between forearms and chest. As eye-hand coordination improves, the child stands in a stationary position and reaches in front of his/her body with arms held straight to catch the ball in both hands. A mature pattern develops with stepping toward the airborne ball, reaching and catching the ball in hands with bent arms, and bringing the ball toward the body (absorbing its momentum).

Ways to Practice Catching

1. Sit in a straddle position and roll and catch a ball with a friend.

2. Catch a suspended ball that freely swings in a pendulum-type path.

3. Catch a tossed balloon or balloon ball. (Balloons are softer and move slower than a ball.)

4. Catch a ball that has been bounced (bounce pass).

5. Catch a ball that has been tossed in the air in a slow moving arc to chest height from a distance of 5-6 feet.

6. Catch a ball from further distances, thrown at a higher speed and in varied paths (in front, to the side, high, low).

Helpful Hints

Some children find that clapping their hands once or twice (palms are facing each other) prepares them in a good "ready position" for catching a

49

"Make It Take It" ISBN 0-9664413-4-6   © 1999, L. Cox and T. Lubbers

ball in their hands (vs. trapping it to their chest in which arms are outstretched and palms facing up).

Rolling Balls

Development of Rolling Balls

When a child first attempts to roll a ball, he/she usually sits in a straddle sitting position.   The child pushes the ball away to an empty space or another person. As the child attains the ability to hold/grasp the ball in two hands, he/she makes a forward movement of the ball with release of the ball as hands are outstretched.

In a standing position a child initially places feet side by side with feet apart. Holding the ball between hands, the child swings the ball slightly back between his/her legs (knees may bend a little) and then pushes the ball forward releasing it at ground level with both arms extended/reaching forward.

Next, the child swings the ball from waist height---down and back to a preferred side while bending knees and slightly leaning upper body forward. As the ball (in hands) is moved/swung from at or behind the side to a space in front of the body, it is released toward the ground in desired direction.

INSTRUCTION AND MOVEMENT CHALLENGE PACKET
"Make It Take It" ISBN 0-9664413-4-6   © 1999, L. Cox and T. Lubbers
This page is reproducible

Kicking Balls

Development of Kicking

A child is ready to begin the skill of kicking shortly after he/she is able to run and when able to balance on one leg momentarily.

 Initially a child uses a pushing action with his/her leg (sometimes nudges it or runs against it in a haphazard manner). The knee may bend and then straighten after the kick depending on the development of balance. A child may use either foot for kicking but will develop a preference when he/she figures out where to place the support (non-kicking) foot. Beginning kicks usually have little upper body movement or coordination.

In a more functional stage of kicking, the child lifts the kicking leg backward and upward in preparation for the kick and swings the leg forward with the knee straightening before touching the ball. The kicking leg continues forward after touching the ball and the arm opposite the support foot begins to reach forward (arm opposition). In the early stages, the part of the foot that contacts the ball is mostly by chance and relates to where the child places the support foot. The child contacts the ball with instep (inside) of the foot if the support foot is close to the ball. The child contacts the ball with toe if the support foot is far behind the ball.

Development of a higher level pattern of kicking occurs when the child takes one or more steps toward the ball. The increased body motion before the kick and the straightened leg before the kick contributes to a more forceful kick (ball goes further). Running and kicking emerge. When the support foot is placed near the ball, greater arm-leg opposition occurs (i.e. left foot placed near the ball with right arm forward). After the foot contacts the ball, the kicking leg continues forward. In a higher level pattern, the kicking foot may swing in an upward arc with contact of the ball below its center so that the ball goes up in the air as well as forward.

INSTRUCTION AND MOVEMENT CHALLENGE PACKET
"Make It Take It" ISBN 0-9664413-4-6   © 1999, L. Cox and T. Lubbers
This page is reproducible

Ways to Practice Kicking

1.   Practice kicking an imaginary ball. The child may want to look in a mirror while doing this.

2.   Use support by a person i.e. hand(s) held or support at waist.

3.   Use support by holding on to an object i.e. chair, wall, table.

4.   Use different sizes and densities of balls. (Balloon balls, Nerf™ balls and beach balls are less threatening than the heavier playground or soccer balls.)

5.   Kick a ball that is hanging just above the ground.

6.   Kick the ball with each foot.

7.   Kick while moving through space.

INSTRUCTION AND MOVEMENT CHALLENGE PACKET
"Make It Take It" ISBN 0-9664413-4-6   © 1999, L. Cox and T. Lubbers
This page is reproducible

CREATING MOVEMENT WITH BEANBAGS

A Collection of Movement Challenges

Beanbags are small enough to carry in a pocket, purse, or backpack and can be readily available to play with. A new location, a friend to play with, different shapes or number of beanbags all might stimulate a variety of ways to play with them.

Kit Contents

1. **Container**

   Ziplock™-type bag, cloth bag, or box

2. **Equipment**

   Two or more beanbags

3. **Instruction and Movement Challenge Packet**

   Decorative "cover page" (you may wish to laminate)

   Instructional pages that explain what children will gain, safety precautions, and hints on how you can help

   Movement challenge pages

Beanbag Construction

1. Cut two pieces of fabric of same size and shape (i.e. square, rectangle, circle, triangle).

2. Put right sides of fabric together and sew around all sides leaving a two inch opening. A double seam is recommended.

3. Turn fabric right side out.

4. Fill beanbag with birdseed, dried beans, popcorn or rice. Different filling material provides a variety of experiences.

5. Sew or top stitch to close the filling hole.

CREATING MOVEMENT WITH BEANBAGS

A Collection of Movement Challenges

Beanbags are small enough to carry in a pocket, purse, or backpack and can be readily available to play with. A new location, a friend to play with, different shapes or number of beanbags all might stimulate a variety of ways to play with them.

INSTRUCTION AND MOVEMENT CHALLENGE PACKET
"Make It Take It" ISBN 0-9664413-4-6   Copyright 1999, L. Cox and T. Lubbers

Beanbags: Instructions

What children will gain:

- balance
- eye-hand coordination
- eye-foot coordination
- body/space awareness
- sequencing skills

- cognitive skills
- body control
- physical fitness
- bilateral coordination
- visual tracking

These underlying factors of motor development assist in the building of movement patterns into smooth, efficient motor skills.

Safety:

✓ Children may need direction regarding where a beanbag may be safely thrown.

✓ Children may need assistance in determining a safe amount of space needed for a particular activity.

How you can help:

✓ Encourage eye contact with the beanbag when tossing or catching.

✓ Encourage controlled movements to ensure success by. . .

- using appropriate speed when moving or balancing (especially not going too fast).
- regulating the force of throws.
- regulating the distance the child stands from the target (i.e. begin close to the target) when throwing for accuracy.

INSTRUCTION AND MOVEMENT CHALLENGE PACKET
"Make It Take It" ISBN 0-9664413-4-6   © 1999, L. Cox and T. Lubbers

Beanbags: Movement Challenges

Can you...

- ✓ balance or place your beanbag on your head? Try balancing the beanbag on different parts of the body such as your shoulder, foot, knee, or elbow. What other body parts can you try?

  - balance the beanbag on different body parts while sitting, standing, kneeling, or lying on your side?
  - move (walk, crawl, scoot, duck walk) while balancing the beanbag on different parts of your body?

- ✓ hold the beanbag in your right hand and kick your right leg up and touch your toes to the beanbag? Do the same for the left hand kicking the left leg up or kicking across left foot to right hand, etc.

- ✓ pass the beanbag around your waist from one hand to the other in a clockwise direction? Pass it the other direction (counterclockwise).

- ✓ pass the beanbag behind your neck and under your chin? Pass it the other direction.

- ✓ pass the beanbag from hand to hand, in a figure-eight pattern between and around your knees?

- ✓ place the beanbag on the floor and make a bridge over the beanbag by having four parts of your body touch the floor?

  - make a bridge using only three parts of your body?
  - make a long bridge? A wide bridge? A high bridge? A narrow bridge?

- ✓ pass the beanbag back and forth between left and right hands?

INSTRUCTION AND MOVEMENT CHALLENGE PACKET
"Make It Take It" ISBN 0-9664413-4-6   © 1999, L. Cox and T. Lubbers
This page is reproducible

✓ toss the beanbag back and forth between your left and right hand? How far apart can you move your hands and still be able to do this?

✓ drop the beanbag with one hand and catch it with the other hand?

✓ throw the beanbag up in the air and catch it with both hands? Or catch it in one hand?

With a friend can you...

✓ pass a beanbag back and forth in time to a rhythm? (say a rhyme, sing a song, or listen to recorded music)

✓ stand back to back and pass the beanbag around both partners from hand to hand as quickly as possible?

✓ stand back to back and pass the beanbag between legs to your friend who returns it over head? How fast can you do this?

✓ play catch using an underhand throw? Begin by standing close to your friend and increase distance as skill improves.

- play catch using an overhand throw?
- play catch varying the kinds of throws between underhand and overhand?
- catch with one hand or two hands?

Can you...

✓ play beanbag bowling by sliding beanbags across a smooth surface to knock over pins?

- When standing? While sitting? While kneeling? When lying on your stomach?
- When standing close to them? When standing far away?

INSTRUCTION AND MOVEMENT CHALLENGE PACKET
"Make It Take It" ISBN 0-9664413-4-6 © 1999, L. Cox and T. Lubbers
This page is reproducible

To make milk carton bowling pins:
Rinse empty pint, quart, or half-gallon milk cartons. Fold tops down and tape. Have fun decorating them by drawing designs, pictures, numbers, or letters on a sheet of paper. Tape or paste the paper to the carton.

Can you...

✓ throw the beanbag and hit a target?

- using an overhand throw? An underhand throw?
- while standing close to a target? While standing far away?

Examples of objects to use as targets:
- a picture drawn on cardboard or tagboard. Prop against chair or wall.
- wastepaper basket, bucket, or bowl
- pillow
- laundry basket
- cookie sheet, plastic coffee can lid, paper plate
- empty box
- chair cushion

Objects could be placed at varying heights, such as on a stool. You might want to assign a point value to each target. Take turns throwing beanbags at the targets. You might want to play until a predetermined point total is reached.

INSTRUCTION AND MOVEMENT CHALLENGE PACKET
"Make It Take It" ISBN 0-9664413-4-6   © 1999, L. Cox and T. Lubbers
This page is reproducible

With a friend(s) can you...

✓ play the game, **HELP YOUR FRIEND:** Have each person place a beanbag on their head and walk around the room. If a beanbag falls off the head, that person must "freeze" (stand still) until a friend picks up the beanbag and places it back on the head of the person who lost it.

✓ toss the beanbag back and forth to each other while you stand still and your friend runs around you in a circle?

✓ toss the beanbag back and forth with one person lying on their back on the floor and the other person standing? Or, try tossing and catching the beanbag while in other positions such as kneeling, lying on side, or squatting?

✓ play a game of catch called **MOVE BACK:** Begin by standing face to face with your friend about two feet apart. Each time the beanbag is caught successfully, the person receiving the beanbag should take one step backward. Each time the beanbag is not caught, the person receiving the beanbag should take one step forward. How far apart can you get?

Can you...

✓ swing your leg forward and backward with the beanbag on your instep?

✓ stand on one foot and reach down to pick up a beanbag that is on the floor without losing your balance?

✓ sit with beanbag on head and get up without using hands and without dropping beanbag?

INSTRUCTION AND MOVEMENT CHALLENGE PACKET
"Make It Take It" ISBN 0-9664413-4-6   © 1999, L. Cox and T. Lubbers
This page is reproducible

✓ toss the beanbag in the air, touch a body part (knee, head, shoulder, or toe) and catch the beanbag?

✓ toss the beanbag to your right side and move sideways to catch it?

✓ toss the beanbag behind you and move backwards to catch it?

✓ place your beanbag on head, tilt your head, and catch the beanbag in your hands as it falls?

✓ toss the beanbag in the air, clap your hands one or more times, and catch the beanbag?

With a friend, can you...

✓ play towel catch?

> Have each person hold opposite ends of a towel. Place a beanbag in the center of the towel. Lift the towel to toss the beanbag into the air and catch it on the towel. You will need a large space for this activity.

- by tossing the beanbag high in the air and catching it on the towel?
- while in different positions such as sitting or kneeling?
- by tossing the beanbag so that you need to move to catch it?
- using a larger or smaller towel?

INSTRUCTION AND MOVEMENT CHALLENGE PACKET
"Make It Take It" ISBN 0-9664413-4-6   © 1999, L. Cox and T. Lubbers
This page is reproducible

Can you...

✓ toss the beanbag under your leg and catch it with two hands? With one hand?

✓ toss the beanbag in the air while squatting and then catch it after standing up?

✓ toss a beanbag in the air, touch the floor and catch the beanbag?

✓ toss the beanbag in the air, turn around, and catch the beanbag?

✓ balance on the right foot and reach down and pick up a beanbag which is placed on the left side of your foot?

✓ hold the beanbag between your feet, jump up and toss the beanbag into your hands?

✓ pick up the beanbag with your feet when you are sitting on the floor with legs straight? With beanbag still between your feet, can you drop the beanbag in a container such as a box, wastepaper basket, or paper grocery bag?

✓ place a beanbag on your right foot, swing leg forward, toss the beanbag from your foot and catch it in both hands or in just your left hand? Or, toss the beanbag with your left foot and catch it in your right hand?

✓ toss the beanbag in the air and touch two different body parts (foot and shoulder) and catch the beanbag?

✓ hold the beanbag at arms length in front of your body with palm up, quickly withdraw hand from under the beanbag and catch it in a palms down stroke before it falls to the floor?

INSTRUCTION AND MOVEMENT CHALLENGE PACKET
"Make It Take It" ISBN 0-9664413-4-6   © 1999, L. Cox and T. Lubbers

✓ throw the beanbag and catch it on a different body part such as your elbow, back, stomach, or head?

✓ hold the beanbag in your right hand over and behind your head, drop the beanbag and catch it with your left hand?

With a friend can you...

✓ play catch using a sock ball?

> To make a sock ball, place a beanbag in the toe of an old nylon stocking or knee high tube sport sock. Tie a string or rubber band just above the beanbag.

- by throwing it overhand? Underhand?
- by holding the beanbag part of the sock ball before throwing? By holding the end of the sock before throwing?
- by hiking the sock ball like a football?
- by throwing it for distance?
- by throwing it for accuracy at a target?

INSTRUCTION AND MOVEMENT CHALLENGE PACKET
"Make It Take It" ISBN 0-9664413-4-6   © 1999, L. Cox and T. Lubbers
This page is reproducible

CREATING MOVEMENT WITH BUBBLES

A Collection of Movement Challenges

Soap bubbles are fascinating for young children. Their colorfulness in sunlight, their floating movements, and the sudden popping, delight young and old alike.

Kit Contents

1. Container

Ziplock™-type bag, cloth bag, or box

2. Equipment

Bubble solution in a non-breakable container. Because the container can become sticky, you may wish to put it in another Ziplock™-type bag and/or consider purchasing the spill-proof containers of bubble solution.

One or two bubble wands

3. Instructions and Movement Challenge Packet

Decorative "cover page" (may wish to laminate)

Bubble solutions

Bubbling tips

Instructional pages that explain what children will gain, safety precautions, and hints on how you can help

Movement challenge pages

Bubble Solutions

Humidity in the air (higher is better), temperature, sky conditions (sunlight weakens bubbles), type of wand used, and the amount of wind outdoors affect bubble formation. The amount of any one ingredient may need to be increased or decreased for successful bubble formation. Some basic recipes for bubble solutions are included as a starting point for hours of soap bubble fun.

Bubble solution containers may include ice cream buckets, cake pans, or plastic wash tubs.

Recipe #1
1 cup of Dawn or Joy dish soap (do not substitute for these brands)
8 cups of water
3 tablespoons of glycerin (available in drug stores)

Recipe #2
2 cups of Dawn or Joy dish soap (do not substitute for these brands)
6 cups of water
$\frac{3}{4}$ cup of Karo syrup

Recipe #3
2 cups of Dawn or Joy dish soap (do not substitute for these brands)
4 cups of warm water
1 package unflavored gelatin
>   **Note:** Solution thickens over time. Success is best if solution is used soon after mixing.

Bubbling Tips

1. Avoid stirring the bubble solution while dipping wand. Stirring creates foam that won't adhere to wand.

2. Scrape off any foam that develops with tagboard or a stiff card.

3. Keep solution clean. Be careful not to get grass, dirt, etc., in the solution.

4. Have a bucket of water available to rinse hands and bubble makers.

5. Try making bubbles at night by moonlight. Or, make bubbles on a very cold winter day. Bubbles may freeze if the temperature is below zero and shatter when they reach the ground.

6. You may wish to hose down your grass if there is a large amount of bubble solution on it.

Types of Bubble Wands and Construction

Many different kinds of bubble wands are commercially available. Small, plastic wands are generally included in small bottles of store bought bubble solution. Bubble wands in many different shapes that are attached to a large stick can be found in many toy or discount stores. Multi-holed wands capable of making many bubbles of various sizes are fun to use. Commercially available large wands made out of a stick with upholstery braid on a movable slider make giant size bubbles. This type of bubble wand requires more coordination and skill to use. In addition, many different kinds of bubble wands can be made at home. You may wish to try any of the following bubble wands.

Paper Cup and Straw Wand

Supplies: 1 styrofoam or paper cup
$\frac{1}{2}$ plastic straw

Directions: Push an end of the straw through the small side of the cup so that the end is inside the cup. Dip the lip of the cup in bubble solution. Blow through the straw with the lip end (part of the cup with the bubble solution) down to make a bubble.

String and Straws

Supplies: 2 straws
1 yard of white string

Directions: Put the string through both straws. Tie the two ends of the string together to form a circle. Hold one straw in each hand and dip the string into the bubble solution. Be careful not to move your fingers or the bubble membrane will pop. To form the bubble, hold the straws into the wind with outstretched hands perpendicular to the ground and quickly bring the straws toward you. To release the bubble from the string, bring the two straws together.

Pipe Cleaner Wands

Supplies: Two or more pipe cleaners

Directions: Bend pipe cleaner into your choice of shapes (for example: heart, square, triangle). Attach another pipe cleaner to use as a handle. Dip wand into solution and wave it in the air or blow on bubble membrane to form bubble.

Plastic Berry Box Wands

Supplies: One plastic lattice box (the kind that strawberries frequently come in)

Directions: Hold box on sides. Dip bottom of box in bubble solution. Wave in air to form many small bubbles.

Plastic Ring Wands

Supplies: Plastic rings that hold a six-pack of soda pop together

Directions: Hold plastic rings on side and dip in bubble solution. Wave in air to form many bubbles. You may want to clip a "pinch-type" clothes pin to the plastic rings as a handle.

Other Bubble Wands:

- toilet paper tubes
- coffee can lids with centers cut out
- paper cups with bottoms cut out
- canning jar lids

CREATING MOVEMENT WITH BUBBLES

A Collection of Movement Challenges

Soap bubbles are fascinating for young children. Their colorfulness in sunlight, their floating movements, and the sudden popping, delight young and old alike.

INSTRUCTION AND MOVEMENT CHALLENGE PACKET
"Make It Take It" ISBN 0-9664413-4-6   Copyright 1999, L. Cox and T. Lubbers

Bubbles: Instructions

What children will gain:

- eye-hand coordination
- eye-foot coordination
- balance
- bilateral coordination
- visual tracking
- body/space awareness
- body control
- physical fitness
- sequencing skills
- midline crossing

Safety:

✓ Promptly wipe up spills of bubble solution.

✓ Be aware that ground and floor surfaces become very slippery when wet. Rotate to different play areas to avoid one area getting too slippery.

✓ Avoid getting bubble solution in eyes. If solution gets in eyes, flush immediately with cold water.

How you can help:

✓ Encourage visually focusing on or tracking the bubbles' flight pattern

✓ Provide experiences in both blowing and popping the bubbles

✓ Stress controlled movements

INSTRUCTION AND MOVEMENT CHALLENGE PACKET
"Make It Take It" ISBN 0-9664413-4-6   © 1999, L. Cox and T. Lubbers
This page is reproducible

Bubble Solutions

Humidity in the air (higher is better), temperature, sky conditions (sunlight weakens bubbles), type of wand used, and the amount of wind outdoors affect bubble formation. The amount of any one ingredient may need to be increased or decreased for successful bubble formation. Some basic recipes for bubble solutions are included as a starting point for hours of soap bubble fun.

Bubble solution containers may include ice cream buckets, cake pans, or plastic wash tubs.

Recipe #1
1 cup of Dawn or Joy dish soap (do not substitute for these brands)
8 cups of water
3 tablespoons of glycerin (available in drug stores)

Recipe #2
2 cups of Dawn or Joy dish soap (do not substitute for these brands)
6 cups of water
¾ cup of Karo syrup

Recipe #3
2 cups of Dawn or Joy dish soap (do not substitute for these brands)
4 cups of warm water
1 package unflavored gelatin
> **Note:** Solution thickens over time. Success is best if solution is used soon after mixing.

INSTRUCTION AND MOVEMENT CHALLENGE PACKET
"Make It Take It" ISBN 0-9664413-4-6   © 1999, L. Cox and T. Lubbers
This page is reproducible

Bubbling Tips

1. Avoid stirring the bubble solution while dipping wand. Stirring creates foam that won't adhere to wand.

2. Scrape off any foam that develops with tagboard or a stiff card.

3. Keep solution clean. Be careful not to get grass, dirt, etc., in the solution.

4. Have a bucket of water available to rinse hands and bubble makers.

5. Try making bubbles at night by moonlight. Or, make bubbles on a very cold winter day. Bubbles may freeze if the temperature is below zero and shatter when they reach the ground.

6. You may wish to hose down your grass if there is a large amount of bubble solution on it.

INSTRUCTION AND MOVEMENT CHALLENGE PACKET
"Make It Take It" ISBN 0-9664413-4-6   © 1999, L. Cox and T. Lubbers

Bubbles: Movement Challenges

To get bubble solution on wands, <u>dip</u> wand in the solution and then lift wand up over the container of solution to allow excess to drip off.

For the following activities, the parent/caregiver should try to blow just one bubble at a time. Many times, when children are given too many stimuli (such as many bubbles), they have difficulty focusing their attention on a specific task and tend to use more uncontrolled movements.

Can you break the bubble...

- ✓ by poking it with your index finger as it floats in the air? Poking with your thumb? Poking with your little finger? Poking with a finger on your non-dominant hand?

- ✓ by clapping it between your hands?

- ✓ by kicking it with one foot? (Often times, children try to kick the bubble when it is still high in the air. Encourage the child to wait until the bubble floats below waist level before trying to kick it.)

- ✓ by using various body parts? Break the bubble with your elbow, knee, or head. What other body parts can you use to break the bubble?

- ✓ when in a crab position? To assume a crab position, sit on the floor  with your knees bent, feet flat on the floor, palms on the floor behind body. Lift stomach. While in a crab position, try to break the bubble by kicking it with a foot, hitting it with your hand, or moving and breaking it with your stomach.

- ✓ with one hand while you are in a wheelbarrow position? Hold the child's feet or thighs, or put his/her feet up on a low object such as a step, inverted bucket, or chair. Hands should be on the ground with elbows straight but not locked.

INSTRUCTION AND MOVEMENT CHALLENGE PACKET
"Make It Take It" ISBN 0-9664413-4-6   © 1999, L. Cox and T. Lubbers
This page is reproducible

✓ while in different positions such as kneeling, sitting, or laying on your back?

✓ by jumping up and breaking a bubble that is floating over your head?

✓ by throwing a ball at it? For a ball, a crumpled piece of newspaper could be used.

✓ by hitting it with a paper towel roll or paper plate that is held in your hand?

✓ by pinching it between your thumb and index finger?

When the child does well with activities in which just one bubble is blown at a time, try blowing many bubbles at the same time.

Can you break the bubbles by...

✓ clapping them between your hands? How many bubbles can you break?

✓ using a sequence of body parts or sides of body?

- poking with the index finger of alternating hands? (First break a bubble with right index finger, then break one with left index finger, and then with right index finger again.) How many bubbles can be broken following this pattern?
- clapping one bubble between your hands, and then kicking and breaking two bubbles?
- hitting two bubbles with a piece of rolled up newspaper and then breaking one bubble by hitting it with your knee?

INSTRUCTION AND MOVEMENT CHALLENGE PACKET
"Make It Take It" ISBN 0-9664413-4-6   © 1999, L. Cox and T. Lubbers
This page is reproducible

Can you...

- ✓ run and hold a bubble wand in a hand out to the side to make a stream of bubbles?

- ✓ spin in a circle and make a tornado of bubbles around you?

Can the child blow...

- ✓ a large bubble? many large bubbles?

- ✓ a small bubble? many small bubbles?

- ✓ a bubble that floats high in the air?

- ✓ a bubble that stays close to the ground?

- ✓ a bubble with a wand held in one hand and catch it on a wand held in the other hand?

- ✓ a bubble with a wand held in the right hand, then transfer the wand to the left hand and catch the bubble?

- ✓ many bubbles and catch three or more bubbles on that same wand? How many bubbles can you catch?

INSTRUCTION AND MOVEMENT CHALLENGE PACKET
"Make It Take It" ISBN 0-9664413-4-6   © 1999, L. Cox and T. Lubbers

CREATING MOVEMENT WITH FISH

A Collection of Movement Challenges

Children enjoy participation in this play scenario of a favorite recreational activity. Using the fishing pole with the magnet as bait, children try to "catch fish" by touching the magnet to the fish. This activity provides many options for cognitive as well as motor challenges.

Kit Contents

1. Container

Ziplock™-type bag, cloth bag, or box

2. Equipment

One or two sets of fishing equipment (pole with fish)

Instructions for making magnet fishing equipment (optional)

Dice for number and math concept activities (optional)

3. Instructions and Movement Challenge Packet

Decorative "cover page" (you may wish to laminate)

Instructional pages that explain what children will gain, safety precautions, and hints on how you can help

Movement challenge pages

Pole and Fish Construction

Fishing Pole:

Cut a wooden dowel, piece of plumbers pipe (PVC), or other plastic pole to desired length. Attach string to pole by tieing, taping, or drilling hole in pole and threading the string through. Attach or tie a magnet to the end of the string.

Fish:

1. *Pattern:* A sample fish pattern is included or you can design your own. Fish notepads may also be found in stationery stores.

2. *Materials:* Fish made out of paper, tagboard, or cardboard. For durability, paper or tagboard fish can be laminated or covered with clear contact paper. Or, fish pictures can be painted or pasted on metal lids from frozen juice cans.

3. *Decorating:* Fabric can be glued to cardboard fish to provide a variety of colors and textures. Or, students may color or paint fish.

4. *Magnet Attraction Materials To Use With Paper, Tagboard, or Cardboard Fish:* Securely glue or tie at the mouth of a fish a piece of metal material that can be purchased in strips from a fabric, stationery, craft, or hobby store or attach a paper clip at the mouth of each fish. Paper clips may need securing by tape on the backside of the fish.

5. *Academic Concept Reinforcement:* To provide reinforcement of various academic skills, fish can be made in different sizes, in different colors, and with numbers or letters written on them. An uppercase letter on large fish and a lowercase letter on small fish could be written.

CREATING MOVEMENT WITH FISH

A Collection of Movement Challenges

Children enjoy participation in this play scenario of a favorite recreational activity. Using the fishing pole with the magnet as bait, children try to "catch fish" by touching the magnet to the fish. This activity provides many options for cognitive as well as motor challenges.

INSTRUCTION AND MOVEMENT CHALLENGE PACKET
"Make It Take It" ISBN 0-9664413-4-6   Copyright 1999, L. Cox and T. Lubbers

Fishing: Instructions

What children will gain:

- eye-hand coordination
- midline crossing
- balance
- sequencing

- body/space awareness
- body control
- cognitive skills

These underlying factors of motor development assist in the building of motor patterns into smooth, efficient motor skills.

Safety:

✓ Children may need help or reminders in managing their fishing pole to avoid touching other people, objects, or preventing getting their lines tangled.

✓ Adults should closely supervise children if they are standing on an object such as a chair or stool. The object that the child is standing on should be stable and secure.

✓ Adults should periodically check that the small magnetic strips and paper clips stay firmly attached to the fish. Small, detached, pieces should be immediately picked up so that small children or pets will not put them in their mouths.

How you can help:

✓ Encourage children to move with slow, controlled movements.

✓ Encourage children to adjust body position for balance when reaching for the fish. You may want to suggest to the child that he/she put an arm out to the side to assist in maintaining a balanced position.

INSTRUCTION AND MOVEMENT CHALLENGE PACKET
"Make It Take It" ISBN 0-9664413-4-6   © 1999, L. Cox and T. Lubbers

✓ Shorten the length of the pole and/or string may make catching the fish easier for children who are having difficulty.

✓ Increase the distance between the child and the fish will increase the challenge for more highly skilled children.

Balance Activities

Creativity in using different surfaces and body positions can help promote balance development. Some possibilities include:

- ✓ using uneven surfaces such as pillows or air mattresses to fish from

- ✓ limiting the base of support by having the child stand on a small object such as a phone book, low stool, or a 4 x 4 board

- ✓ varying the position the child is in when catching the fish (sitting, standing, tall kneeling, or standing on one foot)

- ✓ placing fish far away from the child so they must stretch to reach them

- ✓ creating a favorite fishing spot with bridges, rocks, islands, or docks. Two ropes, strings, a long 2 x 4 piece of wood, or two pieces of masking tape placed in parallel lines on the floor could be a bridge or dock from which to fish. Telephone books, carpet squares, or small pieces of board can be rocks to step on or islands on which to stand.

Crossing the Midline Activities

Crossing the midline means performing an activity with one hand on the opposite side of the body, i.e. using the right hand to manipulate objects on the left side of the body or using the left hand on the right side of the body. Developing the ability to cross the midline is necessary for a child to perform smooth movements and is felt to improve a child's performance when crossing visual fields when reading and copying written work.

INSTRUCTION AND MOVEMENT CHALLENGE PACKET
"Make It Take It" ISBN 0-9664413-4-6   © 1999, L. Cox and T. Lubbers
This page is reproducible

Crossing the midline activities might include:

- ✓ placing the fish on the non dominant side of the body. The child should reach across his or her body with the pole to catch the fish.

- ✓ reaching across the body to place the fish in a bucket (after the fish is caught).

Hand and Object Control Activities

For development of hand and object control, try different ways to take the fish off of the fishing pole by:

- ✓ having the adult take the fish off the fishing line while the child steadies the pole

- ✓ having the child hold the pole in one hand and take the fish off with the other hand

- ✓ having the child move the pole with the fish attached to a bucket or other container which is placed on the floor. The child could shake the pole until the fish falls off the magnet into the bucket.

- ✓ having the child roll the pole in his/her hand thereby rolling the string around the pole. Continue rolling until the magnet and fish are next to the pole and the string is wrapped around the pole. The child can then take the fish off the pole.

Sequencing Activities

The ability to sequence or follow a series of directions or a pattern is an important skill for a child to learn because it involves memory skills as well as proper ordering. Children must frequently follow a series of directions from adults such as "put on your pajamas, brush your teeth, and go to bed."

89

"Make It Take It" ISBN 0-9664413-4-6   © 1999, L. Cox and T. Lubbers

Teachers may give sequences of directions such as "cut out the flower, cover it with glue, and then sprinkle with glitter." Academic skills such as learning to spell words, rote counting, and putting words together to form sentences, also require sequencing abilities. Sequencing skills could be improved by:

✓ having the child verbally repeat out loud the sequence of fish he/she is to pick up

✓ using cue words such as first _____, then _____.

✓ giving the child a sequence of colors, sizes, letters, or numbers of fish you want to be caught. For example, say, "first pick up a green fish, then a blue fish." Or, use a sequence of sizes, i.e. first catch a big fish, then a small fish, then a medium fish.

✓ letting the child catch several fish in any order that he/she chooses. Then ask, "which color fish did you pick up first, second, or third?"

Size, Color, and Letter Concept Activities

While working on motor skills, fishing activities can also be used to reinforce learning academic concepts. For these activities, fish are needed that are different sizes, colors, and that have a specific letter of the alphabet written on them.

To reinforce size concepts:

✓ Specify the size of the fish the child should catch, i.e. "catch all the small fish."

✓ Let the child catch any fish and tell which size was caught.

✓ Have children catch fish in order of size from smallest to largest.

To reinforce color concepts:

✓ Specify the color of the fish the child should catch i.e. "catch all the blue fish".

✓ Let the child catch any fish and then tell what color fish was caught.

To reinforce letter concepts:

✓ Tell the child to pick up a fish with a specific letter on it, i.e. "catch the fish with the letter 'B' on it."

✓ Let the child catch any fish and then tell what letter is on the fish that was caught.

✓ Have the child catch fish in alphabetical order, i.e. first the "*A*," then the "*B*," etc.

✓ Have the child catch any fish with an upper case letter and then catch the fish with the corresponding lower case letter.

✓ Children who are learning to spell can pick up fish with the appropriate letters to spell a word such as their name.

INSTRUCTION AND MOVEMENT CHALLENGE PACKET
"Make It Take It" ISBN 0-9664413-4-6 © 1999, L. Cox and T. Lubbers
This page is reproducible

Number and Math Concept Activities:

 Fishing activities can be used to reinforce number and math skills while also improving balance, eye-hand coordination, and object control skills. For these activities, fish are needed with a different number written on each fish.

To reinforce number identification and counting skills:

✓ Tell the child to pick up a fish with a specific number on it, i.e. "pick up the fish with the number 6 on it."

✓ Let the child catch any fish and then tell what number is on the fish.

✓ Have the child pick up the fish in numerical order, i.e. first pick up the fish with the number 1 on it, then the fish with the number 2 on it, etc.

✓ Give the child some objects such as blocks or spoons. Have them count the objects and then catch the fish with the corresponding number on it.

✓ Roll dice and pick up the fish with the appropriate number on it.

Other number/math concepts:

✓ Have the child pick up numbers in his/her phone number or house number.

✓ To reinforce math facts, give the child a math problem such as 4 + 5 and have the child fish for the correct answer (9). For problems requiring a two-digit answer (i.e. 5 + 7), the child could pick up two fish, (the fish with the "1" and the fish with the "2" for the answer "12."

INSTRUCTION AND MOVEMENT CHALLENGE PACKET
"Make It Take It" ISBN 0-9664413-4-6   © 1999, L. Cox and T. Lubbers

✓ Enlarge or reduce the size of the fish and award different point values for different size fish. Place fish with more points in a location where it is more difficult to catch them. (i.e. farther away from the child).

Fishing with Fitness Activities:

On the bottom (reverse side of each fish), write or attach with a paper clip an activity that the child can do. When the child catches a fish, the specified activity can be read by the adult or child. Examples of possible activities are:

✓ a particular fitness exercise (i.e. 5 curl-ups, or 10 skiers jumps)

✓ a locomotor movement (i.e. skip to the _____ and then hop back)

Fishing with Holiday/Seasonal Activities

Valentines Day Fishing

✓ Construct fish using heart shapes in red, pink, and white colors.

✓ Give the child a sequence of colors to follow when picking up the fish, (i.e. first pick up a white fish, then a red fish, then a pink fish).

✓ Place a different letter on each fish: v-a-l-e-n-t-i-n-e. Have the child pick up the fish in the order that spell the word, "valentine."

INSTRUCTION AND MOVEMENT CHALLENGE PACKET
"Make It Take It" ISBN 0-9664413-4-6   © 1999, L. Cox and T. Lubbers
This page is reproducible

Winter/Ice Fishing

✓ Make "ice" using large sheets of white paper or old bed sheet with a hole cut in middle (fishing hole).

✓ Place the "ice" on floor; put fish in "fishing hole."

✓ Children can sit on overturned bucket or T-stool "to fish."

✓ Construct an ice fishing house from an old appliance box (make door and windows) for children to sit in and "ice fish."

INSTRUCTION AND MOVEMENT CHALLENGE PACKET
"Make It Take It" ISBN 0-9664413-4-6   © 1999, L. Cox and T. Lubbers

CREATING MOVEMENT WITH HOOPS

A Collection of Movement Challenges

Hoops provide children with the opportunity to enhance skill development, promote creative play, and increase physical fitness. They can be used to explore movement or for cooperative or competitive activities. Hoops can be used by oneself, with a partner, or with a group of people.

Kit Contents

1. Container

Ziplock™-type bag, cloth bag, or box

2. Equipment

Commercially available hula hoop or hoop piece segments. Include enough pieces to assemble to a 36 to 48 inch hoop.

or

Homemade hoop made from plumber pipe & dowel/coupler.

Optional: Beanbags for Beanbag Scramble game

3. Instructions and Movement Challenge Packet

Decorative "cover page" (may wish to laminate)

Instructional pages that explain what children will gain, safety precautions, and hints on how you can help

Movement challenge pages

A low cost, durable hoop can be made from 1/2 inch wide (or larger size if you wish) piece of flexible plastic pipe/plumbing pipe and a "coupler" made from a 1/2-5/8 inch wide piece of wooden dowel.

Hoops can be made to any desired size. Hoops with two foot diameter need a 75" length of plastic pipe and hoops with three foot diameter need a 113" length. The dowel should be 3"-4" long.

Each end of the dowel is inserted in each end of the pipe. If the dowel doesn't fit into the pipe, put the ends of the pipe in hot water for several minutes which allows it to expand for easier insertion. The hoop can be decorated with colored tape if desired.

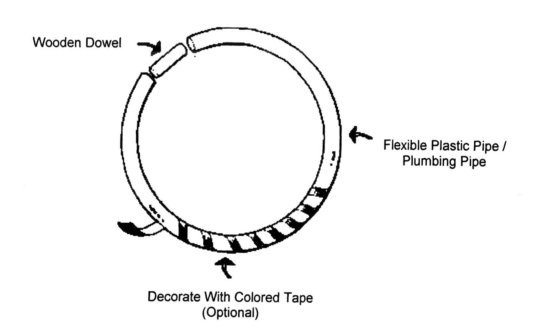

Wooden Dowel

Flexible Plastic Pipe /
Plumbing Pipe

Decorate With Colored Tape
(Optional)

CREATING MOVEMENT WITH HOOPS

A Collection of Movement Challenges

Hoops provide children with the opportunity to enhance skill development, promote creative play, and increase physical fitness. They can be used to explore movement or for cooperative or competitive activities. Hoops can be used by oneself, with a partner, or with a group of people.

INSTRUCTION AND MOVEMENT CHALLENGE PACKET
"Make It Take It" ISBN 0-9664413-4-6   Copyright 1999, L. Cox and T. Lubbers

Hoops: Instructions

What children will gain:

- eye-hand coordination
- eye-foot coordination
- creative expression
- object manipulation skills
- cognitive concept development
  (inside, outside, high, low)
- locomotor skills

- body/space awareness
- body control
- physical fitness
- sequencing
- balance

Safety:

✓ Allow enough space for movement when using hoops.

How you can help:

✓ Encourage the child to explore, try, and problem solve many different ways to use the hoop.

✓ Encourage the child to control his/her body by using questions such as "can you move without falling? Without bumping into anything? Try moving a little slower."

INSTRUCTION AND MOVEMENT CHALLENGE PACKET
"Make It Take It" ISBN 0-9664413-4-6   © 1999, L. Cox and T. Lubbers

Hoops: Movement Challenges

With the hoop flat on the floor, can you...

✓ put your head inside the hoop? Your toe? Your elbow? Your knee? What other parts of your body can you put inside the hoop?

✓ stand inside the hoop, pick it up and hold it knee high? Waist high? Shoulder high?

✓ stand in front of, behind, in, out, to the right of and to the left of your hoop?

✓ stand inside the hoop, hold it waist high with one hand on each side of the hoop, and walk around the room touching your knee to the hoop on each step?

✓ balance with one foot on the floor outside the hoop and two hands on the floor inside the hoop?

✓ balance with two body parts on the floor outside the hoop and three body parts inside the hoop?

✓ make a bridge over your hoop (pretend pond or lake) by placing two hands on the floor on one side of the hoop and two feet on the floor on the other side? How long can you hold your bridge?

✓ move around your hoop keeping two hands on the floor inside the hoop and two feet on the floor outside the hoop?

✓ do different animal walks around your hoop? Can you be a frog? A rabbit? A crab?

✓ gallop or skip around the outside of the hoop?

✓ stand inside the hoop and balance on one foot? Stoop low while balancing? Stretch high while balancing?

INSTRUCTION AND MOVEMENT CHALLENGE PACKET
"Make It Take It" ISBN 0-9664413-4-6   © 1999, L. Cox and T. Lubbers
This page is reproducible

✓ stand inside your hoop, jump backwards out of your hoop and forward into your hoop? Can you jump sideways in and out of your hoop?

✓ stand outside your hoop and jump into your hoop and land in a low or squat position?

✓ stand inside your hoop and jump four times making each jump a little higher than the previous jump?

✓ jump as far as possible out of your hoop, turn around and jump back into your hoop?

✓ stand outside your hoop, jump and turn half way around before landing inside your hoop?

✓ jump forward around the hoop keeping one foot inside the hoop and the other outside? Jump backward around the hoop with one foot inside and the other outside. Can you do this without touching the hoop?

✓ jump with your feet together around the hoop alternating jumps so that both feet are inside the hoop and then both feet are outside the hoop?

✓ jump very quickly in and out of your hoop? Can you do 15 jumps in 10 seconds? How many times can you jump before becoming tired?

✓ jump in and out of the hoop while counting or reciting the letters of the alphabet? When counting, jump inside the hoop for the odd numbers and outside the hoop for even numbers. When reciting the letters of the alphabet, jump outside the hoop for consonants and inside for vowels.

✓ hop on one foot around the outside of the hoop?

INSTRUCTION AND MOVEMENT CHALLENGE PACKET
"Make It Take It" ISBN 0-9664413-4-6   © 1999, L. Cox and T. Lubbers
This page is reproducible

✓ stand inside your hoop and hop on one foot while turning around in a circle?

✓ hop on one foot in and out of your hoop in different directions such as forward, backward, and sideways?

✓ pretend the hoop is a puddle and run and leap over it?

Can you...

✓ hold the hoop in both hands and stretch it high over your head? Bend low and hold it close to the floor? How low can you hold it without letting it touch the floor?

✓ balance your hoop on your head with the hoop hanging in front of your body? Can you balance the hoop on your head while walking around the room, gym, or play area?

✓ hold the hoop over your head, drop it, and let it fall to the floor without touching your body?

✓ hold the hoop in both hands in front of your body and use it as a steering wheel to drive around the room, gym, or outdoor area?

✓ make letters or numbers using your hoop and body? Can you make a "6," "10," "b," "d," "g," "p," or "Q"?

✓ spin the hoop in a circle like a top or egg beater? How long can you make it spin? How many times can you run, gallop, skip, or hop around the spinning hoop before it stops?

✓ use the hoop like a jump rope? How many times can you turn and jump over the hoop?

INSTRUCTION AND MOVEMENT CHALLENGE PACKET
"Make It Take It" ISBN 0-9664413-4-6   © 1999, L. Cox and T. Lubbers
This page is reproducible

✓ roll the hoop on the floor? How far can you make it roll?

✓ throw the hoop in the air and catch it before it hits the floor?

✓ roll the hoop on the floor and catch it before it falls to the floor?

✓ roll the hoop on the floor, run forward along side of it, and give it small pushes so it doesn't fall over?

✓ roll the hoop and crawl through it while it is moving?

✓ roll the hoop on the floor using backspin so that it rolls back to you? The key to putting backspin on the hoop is to pull down (toward the floor) on the hoop as it is released.

✓ spin the hoop around one arm? Around your neck? Around your knees?

✓ spin the hoop around your waist by moving your hips quickly forward and backward? (the "hula hoop" movement)

✓ place the hoop on the floor and shuffle kick the hoop around the room, gym, or play area with your feet like dribbling a soccer ball?

✓ do a sequence of skills such as jump into the hoop, balance on one foot for 5 seconds, and hop out of the hoop? What other movement sequences can you think of?

With one hoop and a friend can you...

✓ crawl/step through the hoop while your friend holds it perpendicular to the floor? Pretend to be a performing circus animal. Go through the hoop head first, feet first, or back first. Have the friend hold it at different heights.

INSTRUCTION AND MOVEMENT CHALLENGE PACKET
"Make It Take It" ISBN 0-9664413-4-6   © 1999, L. Cox and T. Lubbers

✓ both get inside the hoop (your hoop mobile), hold it waist high, and cooperatively move around the room, play area or outdoors? You will need to move at the same speed.

✓ stand about 5-10 feet apart and roll the hoop back and forth to each other?

✓ stand beside your friend who will roll the hoop away from you. Can you run and catch it? Take turns running to catch the hoop.

✓ run through a hoop that is rolled by your friend?

✓ toss the hoop back and forth and catch it on your arm?

✓ play hoop horseshoes? To do this, place different objects (wastepaper basket, telephone book, chair or stool turned upside down) around the room or play area. Take turns tossing the hoop to see if you can get it around an object. A point value could be assigned to each object.

✓ join hands and spin the hoop around your arms together?

✓ jump or hop through a hoop that is held by your friend? Try holding the hoop different heights off the floor and at different angles. Be sure that your friend is holding the hoop loosely, so that if you hit the hoop, the hoop will fall to the floor to avoid tripping and falling.

✓ take turns jumping into and out of the hoop? To do this, face your friend and hold hands. One person should be standing inside the hoop and the other person outside the hoop. On a designated signal, the person who is standing inside the hoop jumps backward out of the hoop while the person who was standing outside the hoop jumps in. Can you develop a rhythm and do this many times?

INSTRUCTION AND MOVEMENT CHALLENGE PACKET
"Make It Take It" ISBN 0-9664413-4-6   © 1999, L. Cox and T. Lubbers

With hoops and friends can you...

Play the game, **MUSICAL HOOPS:** If you have multiple hoops, then lay them on the floor. Children move (walk, gallop, jump, hop, etc) among the hoops. On a given signal, (i.e. music stops), children step into a hoop. If there aren't enough hoops, children can share. Sometimes children like to pretend the hoops are houses (i.e. on signal, go stand in a house). Hoops could be eliminated for challenge and excitement, but all children should remain in the game to foster cooperation versus competition.

Play the game, **BEANBAG SCRAMBLE:** Place a pile of beanbags (or yarn balls at one end of the room and a hoop(s) at the other end. On a signal children run across the room, pick up one beanbag and run with it to the hoop. . . placing it in the hoop. Continue until all the beanbags are in the hoop.

INSTRUCTION AND MOVEMENT CHALLENGE PACKET
"Make It Take It" ISBN 0-9664413-4-6   © 1999, L. Cox and T. Lubbers
This page is reproducible

CREATING MOVEMENT WITH RACQUETS AND BATS

A Collection of Movement Challenges

From primitive games to highly organized sports, children have naturally created play by hitting an object with a bat or racquet. Activities with bats or racquets can be exploratory in nature or specific towards a sport or organized game. Eye-hand coordination is challenged with such activities.

Kit Contents

1. Container

Ziplock™-type bag, cloth bag, or box

2. Equipment

Striking implements:
- <u>commercially purchased</u> (i.e. lollipop/styrofoam paddles, plastic racquets, foam or plastic bats, fly swatters)
- <u>homemade</u> (i.e. nylon paddles, paper plate paddles, paper sticks, cardboard tubes)

Objects to strike:
- balloons, balloon balls, balls of various sizes and densities
- suspended balls
- larger cloth balls (see directions)
- tennis ball or other small ball tied in a sock or nylon hosiery

Optional: beanbag(s) for selected activities

3. Instructions and Movement Challenge Packet

Decorative "cover page" (may wish to laminate.)

Instructional pages that explain what children will gain, safety precautions, and hints on how you can help

Movement challenge pages

Homemade Racquets and Bats

COATHANGER RACQUET

1. Bend the triangle part of a coat hanger to form a diamond shape for the racquet face.

2. To make the handle bend the hook end of the hanger against the hanger neck (see illustration).

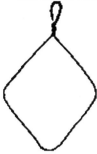

3. Pull a nylon stocking tightly over the diamond frame.

4. Wrap excess nylon around the handle for padding.

5. Wrap the entire handle with tape for padding and safety.

PAPER STICK BAT

1. Roll a section of newspaper into a long tube. The amount of newspaper used will determine how wide (size of diameter) the tube will be.

2. Wrap tape around the newspaper tube at one-inch intervals.

PAPER PLATE RACQUET

1. Any size paper plate will work. If plates are thin, several might be taped together (stacked on top of each other).

2. Children can decorate them with crayons, paint, or markers.

CARDBOARD TUBE BAT

1.   Empty tubes from paper towel rolls or gift wrapping rolls make fun bats.

2.   They can be decorated with colorful tape or with drawings using crayons or markers.

Homemade Suspendable Cloth Balls

1. Make a paper pattern from a section of an old beachball. The pattern should be 1/2"-3/4" wider/bigger than the beachball section for a seam allowance.

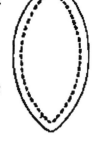

2. Cut out six sections/panels per ball of different colors or prints.

3. Sew sections. Place right sides together and double stitch each seam for strength.

4. Sew a piece of hook Velcro™ (3-4" long) on the right side in the middle of the first section and a piece of pile Velcro™ in the middle and on the right side of the last section to make the closable hole where stuffing can be inserted. (You may wish to sew the Velcro™ on before beginning to sew the sections together.)

5. After all sections are sewn together, turn the ball inside out through the Velcro™ hole so the right side is facing out and seams are inside.

6. Cut two small six-sided shapes (about 2" in diameter) from fabric and fold edges slightly under. Stitch to top and bottom of cloth ball where the "points" of the sections/panels meet.

7. Also, as the top and bottom piece is being sewn in place, sew a cloth loop into the seams at the top. Triple stitch for strength.

To make loop: Fold a 1 x 5" piece of fabric over twice to hide raw edge. Stitch twice on top for reinforcement.

8. The ball can be stuffed with different items for varying grasp/feel such as crumpled newspaper, styro packing pellets/peanuts, crumpled plastic bubble paper, fabric or old nylons, or a beachball (blow up once inside).

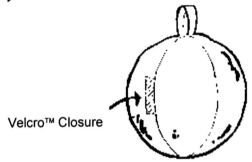

Velcro™ Closure

CREATING MOVEMENT WITH RACQUETS AND BATS

A Collection of Movement Challenges

From primitive games to highly organized sports, children have naturally created play by hitting an object with a bat or racquet. Activities with bats or racquets can be exploratory in nature or specific towards a sport or organized game. Eye-hand coordination is challenged with such activities.

INSTRUCTION AND MOVEMENT CHALLENGE PACKET
"Make It Take It" ISBN 0-9664413-4-6   Copyright 1999, L. Cox and T. Lubbers
This page is reproducible

Racquets and Bats: Instructions

What children will gain:

- eye-hand coordination
- midline crossing
- visual tracking
- cognitive skills

- body/space awareness
- body control
- physical fitness
- sequencing

Children have a natural urge to bat or strike at objects with body parts (i.e. hands or feet) or with an object (i.e. stick, bat, racquet) as part of play. Play experiences with hitting activities are foundational for higher level skills used in low organized games and sports (i.e. tennis, racquetball, handball, badminton, T-ball/baseball, volleyball)

Safety:

✓ Allow sufficient space so that bats and racquets swung in the air will not bump people or things (i.e. when batting or swinging a racquet, people should not stand near)

✓ Allow sufficient space so that objects propelled in the air will not hit anyone or anything

How you can help:

✓ Encourage the child to keep eyes on the object he/she plans to hit (i.e. ball, balloon).

✓ Select larger objects to be hit (balloons, beachball etc.) before trying smaller objects (i.e. tennis ball).

✓ Encourage hitting suspended objects before attempting to hit airborne objects.

114

"Make It Take It" ISBN 0-9664413-4-6   © 1999, L. Cox and T. Lubbers

✓ Use slower moving objects (i.e. balloon, balloon ball) before faster moving objects (balls with more density).

✓ Use hands to hit an object before hitting with a bat or racquet.

✓ Use a bat or racquet with a shorter handle (i.e. lollipop paddle or nylon racquet) before use of a longer handled racquet (i.e. tennis or badminton racquet).

✓ Encourage the child to explore striking with both hands on the "bat or racquet" (encourages midline crossing as well as coordination of right and left hands).

INSTRUCTION AND MOVEMENT CHALLENGE PACKET
"Make It Take It" ISBN 0-9664413-4-6   © 1999, L. Cox and T. Lubbers
This page is reproducible

Racquets and Bats: Movement Challenges

Can you hit a suspended object i.e. balloon or beachball hung by a string from a ceiling hook, doorway, tree branch etc....

...with a body part (elbow, knee, foot, thumb)

...with a racquet or bat

✓ while sitting, tall kneeling, half kneeling, standing, or in wheelbarrow position?

✓ while the ball remains stationary? Or, when it is moving?

✓ using soft or hard hits?

✓ up, down, or to the side?

✓ many consecutive times?

✓ back and forth to a partner?

With a racquet or bat, can you hit a ball from a stationary object i.e. batting T, marker cone, overturned wastebasket, overturned box...

✓ a long distance? High in the air?

✓ straight ahead? To the left? To the right?

✓ at a target?

INSTRUCTION AND MOVEMENT CHALLENGE PACKET
"Make It Take It" ISBN 0-9664413-4-6   © 1999, L. Cox and T. Lubbers
This page is reproducible

Can you hit an airborne/tossed object (i.e. balloon, beach balls, nerf balls, balls of different sizes and densities)...

✓ many times without missing?

✓ a long distance? High in the air?

✓ with a racquet or bat held in your non-dominant hand?

With a friend can you hit/tap/strike an object back and forth to each other (volley)...

✓ many times in a row?

✓ using only one hand? Using both hands?

✓ back and forth over a net?

Can you...

✓ balance an object on your racquet

  - as you move in different directions (forward, backward, in a circle)?
  - on the backhand side of the racquet?
  - as you move the racquet up and down?
  - as you change levels from standing to kneeling?

✓ place an object on the floor and tap or strike it as you move to different locations around the room, gym, or play area?

✓ continually tap or strike an object to yourself

INSTRUCTION AND MOVEMENT CHALLENGE PACKET
"Make It Take It" ISBN 0-9664413-4-6   © 1999, L. Cox and T. Lubbers
This page is reproducible

- alternating forehand and backhand?
- hitting the object in the air with your racquet and then hitting it with the opposite hand (the one not holding the racquet)?
- when changing the racquet from hand to hand?
- when changing levels i.e. moving from standing to sitting?
- bouncing the object on the floor and hitting it again when it rebounds?
- alternately hitting an object up in the air and then down on the floor?
- using different types of hits such as underhand, overhand, backhand?

✓ hit the object against a wall?

✓ hit the object at a target?

Using a racquet and a beanbag, can you...

✓ drop the beanbag from your hand which is held high in the air and catch the beanbag on your racquet that is held in your other hand?

✓ toss the beanbag which is held in your left hand and catch it on your racquet which is held in your right hand?

✓ balance the beanbag on the face of the racquet, toss the beanbag up in the air and catch it on the face of the racquet? You will need to "give" as you catch the beanbag. Repeat, except turn your racquet over (backhand side) and catch the beanbag.

✓ put the beanbag in one hand and the racquet in the other and toss the beanbag from hand to racquet and racquet to hand (like juggling)?

INSTRUCTION AND MOVEMENT CHALLENGE PACKET
"Make It Take It" ISBN 0-9664413-4-6   © 1999, L. Cox and T. Lubbers

CREATING MOVEMENT WITH ROPES

A Collection of Movement Challenges

Ropes are a very versatile piece of equipment. Besides the traditional rope jumping activities, ropes can be used in a number of creative ways to improve balance, fitness, coordination and sense of rhythm. All ages from preschool-aged children with supervision to professional athletes can use ropes for entertainment and challenging skill development. Generally, ropes can be used indoors or out, and require only a small activity space.

Kit Contents

1. Container

Ziplock™-type bag, cloth bag, or box

2. Equipment

One or two ropes seven to eight feet in length. The rope should be flexible, thick, and heavy enough to maintain the momentum when turning. Many kinds of jump ropes are available through catalogues, discount stores, or sporting good stores. You may wish to purchase 3/8 inch to 5/8 inch diameter sash cord.   Dip ends of the rope in melted wax or wrap in tape to prevent fraying. For traditional rope jumping movement challenges, you may wish to use a heavier rope such as a plastic link or licorice jump rope.

3. Instructions and Movement Challenge Packet

Decorative cover page (may wish to laminate)

Instructional pages that explain what children will gain, safety precautions, and hints on how you can help

Movement challenge pages

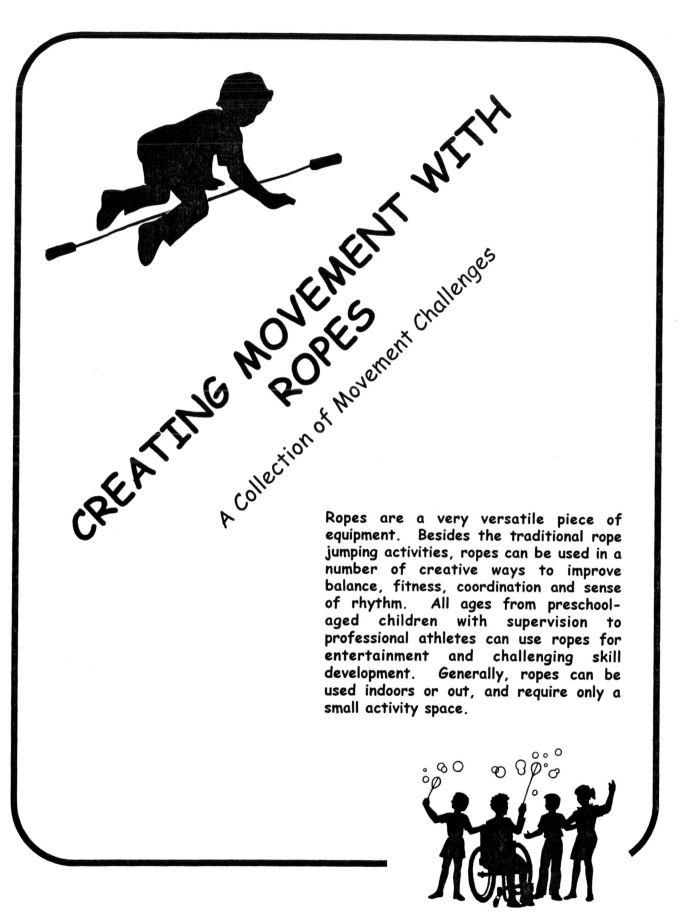

CREATING MOVEMENT WITH ROPES

A Collection of Movement Challenges

Ropes are a very versatile piece of equipment. Besides the traditional rope jumping activities, ropes can be used in a number of creative ways to improve balance, fitness, coordination and sense of rhythm. All ages from preschool-aged children with supervision to professional athletes can use ropes for entertainment and challenging skill development. Generally, ropes can be used indoors or out, and require only a small activity space.

INSTRUCTION AND MOVEMENT CHALLENGE PACKET
"Make It Take It" ISBN 0-9664413-4-6   Copyright 1999, L. Cox and T. Lubbers

Ropes: Instructions

What children will gain:

✿ rhythm skills
✿ locomotor skills
✿ balance
✿ creative expression
✿ bilateral coordination

✿ body/space awareness
✿ body control
✿ physical fitness
✿ cognitive skills
✿ sequencing skills

Safety:

✓ Ropes should not be swung like a whip.

✓ Use ropes on a non-skid surface.

✓ Allow sufficient space for activities.

How you can help:

✓ Encourage a two-foot take-off and landing when jumping. Feet should be slightly apart. Suggest children jump like a rabbit, kangaroo, or grasshopper.

✓ Stress bent knees before take-off and landing when jumping to cushion the shock.

✓ Remind children to land on the balls of their feet when jumping.

✓ Emphasize use of arms when jumping. Swinging arms helps in lifting the body higher and in controlling the direction on the jump. Arms held out to the side assist with balance.

✓ Use an even beat music selection to assist in developing a sense of rhythm when jumping.

INSTRUCTION AND MOVEMENT CHALLENGE PACKET
"Make It Take It" ISBN 0-9664413-4-6   © 1999, L. Cox and T. Lubbers

Ropes: Movement Challenges

With the rope placed in a straight line on the floor, can you...

✓ get in a hands and knees position with right hand and right knee on one side of the rope and left hand and left knee on the other and creep forward without touching the rope with your body? Can you creep backwards without touching the rope?

✓ move the length of the rope like a <u>bear</u>? To do this, straddle the rope with your left foot and left hand on one side of the rope and your right foot and right hand on the other side. Move your left hand and foot forward at the same time and then your right foot and right hand.

✓ place one foot on each side of the rope, squat and jump the length of the rope like a <u>rabbit</u>? To do this, move both hands forward together and then jump both feet forward.

✓ place one foot on each side of the rope and <u>crab walk</u> the length of  the rope? To get into the crab position, sit on the floor with knees bent, feet close to hips, and hands behind you on the floor. Lift hips and hold your body up with your hands and feet. Walk by making small steps with hands and feet.

✓ walk the length of the rope using just two hands and one foot touching the floor like a <u>three-legged dog</u>?

✓ walk on the rope like a tightrope? Walk forward, backward or sideways.

✓ walk forward on the rope with very small steps touching the heel of one foot to the toe of the other?

123

"Make It Take It" ISBN 0-9664413-4-6   © 1999, L. Cox and T. Lubbers

✓ stand with one foot on each side of the rope and do criss-cross walking by stepping and placing your right foot on the left side of the rope and your left foot on the right side of the rope?

✓ make a bridge over the rope by putting two hands on the floor on one side of the rope and two feet on the other side? Can you make your bridge travel by walking your hands and feet the length of the rope?

Also with the rope placed in a line, can you...

✓ jump low over the rope without touching it?

✓ jump high over the rope?

✓ place one foot on each side of the rope so that you are straddling it and jump the length of the rope?

✓ do crouch jumps over the rope? Begin in a squat position and jump sideways back and forth over the rope?

✓ stand with the rope in front of your toes and jump forward and backward over the rope?

✓ jump back and forth over a rope in a specific rhythm such as slow-slow-fast-fast?

✓ jump back and forth across the rope while moving in a backward direction the length of the rope?

✓ straddle the rope with one leg on each side, jump and make a half turn and land facing the opposite direction?

✓ stand straddling the rope, jump, and land with your feet crossed?

✓ hop on one foot back and forth over the rope?

124

"Make It Take It" ISBN 0-9664413-4-6   © 1999, L. Cox and T. Lubbers

With the rope placed in a circle on the floor can you balance...

✓ for ten seconds with two hands inside the circle and one foot outside of the circle?

✓ with only two elbows touching the floor inside the circle, and two knees on the outside of the circle? What other balances can you think of using other parts of your body?

✓ on one foot with your eyes closed while standing inside the circle?

With the rope placed in a circle on the floor, can you...

✓ make your body very small inside the circle?

✓ make a bridge over your circle by placing two hands on the floor on one side of the circle and two feet on the other? Can you make your bridge low, high, narrow, or wide? Can you make your bridge go up and down by bending and straightening your knees and elbows?

✓ place your feet in the circle and walk your hands all around the outside of the circle?

✓ place your hands inside the circle and your feet outside the circle while facing the ceiling (crab walk position) and walk your feet around the outside of the circle?

With the rope placed in a circle on the floor can you move by...

✓ jumping on both feet around the outside of the circle? Can you jump all the way around the outside of your circle in only six jumps? Or five jumps?

INSTRUCTION AND MOVEMENT CHALLENGE PACKET
"Make It Take It" ISBN 0-9664413-4-6 © 1999, L. Cox and T. Lubbers
This page is reproducible

✓ putting one foot inside the circle and the other foot outside the circle and jumping all the way around the circle?

✓ standing inside the circle and doing a sequence of jumps of various heights such as two high jumps followed by a low jump?

✓ jumping three times inside the circle and two times outside the circle? What other jumping patterns or sequences can you think of?

✓ standing in the circle, jumping and turning, so that you land facing the opposite direction?

✓ jumping forward into the circle and backward out of the circle?

✓ hopping on one foot around the outside of the circle?

✓ running and leaping over your circle?

Try these rope games...

LEAP THE SNAKE: Tie one end of the rope around an object such as the leg of a piece of furniture, tree, or doorknob. Have a friend loosely hold the other end of the rope and wiggle it on the floor quickly like a snake. Can you run and leap over the moving rope? If more than one friend is available to play, have each one hold one end of the rope and wiggle it.

JUMP THE SHOT: The "turner" holds one end of the rope in one hand and moves the rope close to the ground turning/pivoting around seated or crouched in one spot (turning clockwise or counterclockwise). The "jumper" stands two or more feet from the turner and jumps over the rope as it goes around in a circle.

126

Rope Jumping

Rope jumping is a very complex skill for a child to learn. It involves coordinated simultaneous movements of arms and legs, proper timing, physical fitness, and a sense of rhythm. Learning to jump rope can be very physically fatiguing, and it requires a high degree of concentration. Frequent, short practice sessions generally are more productive than a long practice period.

How you can help...

✓ Assist the child in determining the correct length of rope to use. To do this, the child should stand on the middle of the rope with feet together. Pull the ends of the rope up along the side of the body. The rope is the correct size if the ends come as high as the armpits. Using a slightly longer rope will provide more maneuverability. A jump rope can be made shorter by wrapping the ends around hands.

✓ Remind the child that the twirl of the rope begins at waist level and not by the shoulders. As skills increase, just circular wrist movements should be used to turn the rope rather than to move the entire arm.

✓ Remind the child to hold elbows close to the body at waist level, with hands held slightly forward and sideways when turning the rope and jumping.

✓ Encourage jumping on the balls of the feet rather than with flat feet.

✓ Stress that jumps should be just high enough for the rope to pass under the feet.

✓ Remind the child to stay in one spot while jumping.

✓ Practice jumping to music with a strong, even beat.

INSTRUCTION AND MOVEMENT CHALLENGE PACKET
"Make It Take It" ISBN 0-9664413-4-6   © 1999, L. Cox and T. Lubbers
This page is reproducible

✓ Encourage good posture when jumping. The head should be up and eyes looking straight forward.

Before attempting to learn to jump rope, the child should have many jumping movement experiences, i.e. jumping over stationary objects, jumping off objects at low or high heights, jumping for distance, etc. After the child has participated in these activities, a variety of techniques can be used to help the child experience early success when learning to jump rope. It may be helpful to practice each skill component (twirling the rope, proper timing, and jumping) independently before attempting to put these skills together to jump rope.

To develop rope twirling...

✓ swing one or both arms in a circular motion at the side of your body. Do not hold a rope—just practice the movement. Begin by making large circles by moving the whole arm. Gradually decrease the size of the circle until the child can just use his/her wrists to make the circles.

✓ place both ends of the rope in one hand. Turn the rope at the side of the body in a steady rhythm. Repeat with the other hand. The adult may need to stand behind the child and physically move the child's hand for a short period of time until the child gets the feel of what to do.

✓ hold one end of the rope in each hand. Position both hands together on the same side of the body. Turn the rope at the side of the body in a steady rhythm.

✓ stand about one foot in front of the child facing him/her. Have the child turn the rope so that it goes over your head. This keeps the child from whipping the rope over his/her head and reinforces controlled twirling.

INSTRUCTION AND MOVEMENT CHALLENGE PACKET
"Make It Take It" ISBN 0-9664413-4-6   © 1999, L. Cox and T. Lubbers
This page is reproducible

✓ have the child hold one end of the rope in each hand with the middle of the rope against heels. Swing the rope overhead and let it stop under toes. Then have the child turn the rope back over the head so it lands back by the heels. Tell the child that you want to have him/her make a rainbow over his/her head with the rope.

To develop proper timing, have the child...

✓ clap the rhythm (when a jump should occur) while you jump rope.

✓ jump to the same rhythm outside of the arc of the rope while you turn and jump over the rope.

✓ place both ends of the rope in one hand and turn the rope at the side of the child's body in a steady rhythm. The child should jump just as the rope hits the ground.

✓ stand about 12" in front and facing you. (or face in the same direction) You can turn the rope and have the child jump with you.

To develop jumping skills...

✓ hold one handle of the rope in each hand with the rope stationary in front of the body. Jump forward and backward over the rope.

✓ same as above, but swing the rope slightly. Increase the arc of the swing gradually until a full turn of the rope can be achieved.

Types of jumps:

✓ Basic two-foot: jump off both feet at the same time over the rope.

INSTRUCTION AND MOVEMENT CHALLENGE PACKET
"Make It Take It" ISBN 0-9664413-4-6   © 1999, L. Cox and T. Lubbers
This page is reproducible

✓ Basic two-foot with rebound: jump off both feet at the same time over the rope. When the rope is overhead, make a small preparatory rebound jump.

✓ Alternate foot: keep one foot in front of the other and shift weight from one foot to the other as the rope passes under the feet.

✓ Hop on right foot.

✓ Hop on left foot.

INSTRUCTION AND MOVEMENT CHALLENGE PACKET
"Make It Take It" ISBN 0-9664413-4-6   © 1999, L. Cox and T. Lubbers

CREATING MOVEMENT WITH SCARVES

A Collection of Movement Challenges

The slow, floating action of scarves makes them an ideal piece of equipment to use in developing eye-hand coordination in young children. Brightly colored, non-threatening scarves that are easy to grasp increase the success rate when teaching catching skills.

Kit Contents

1. Container

Ziplock™-type bag, cloth bag, or box

2. Equipment

Two or three different colored, sheer, lightweight (chiffon fabric), juggling scarves that are 18" to 24" square

3. Instructions and Movement Challenge Packet

Decorative cover page (may wish to laminate)

Instructional pages that explain what children will gain, safety precautions, and hints on how you can help

Movement challenge pages

CREATING MOVEMENT WITH SCARVES

A Collection of Movement Challenges

The slow, floating action of scarves makes them an ideal piece of equipment to use in developing eye-hand coordination in young children. Brightly colored, non-threatening scarves that are easy to grasp increase the success rate when teaching catching skills.

INSTRUCTION AND MOVEMENT CHALLENGE PACKET
"Make It Take It" ISBN 0-9664413-4-6   Copyright 1999, L. Cox and T. Lubbers
This page is reproducible

Scarves: Instructions

What children will gain:

- ✿ eye-hand coordination
- ✿ non-locomotor skills
- ✿ rhythm skills
- ✿ bilateral coordination
- ✿ visual tracking

- ✿ body/space awareness
- ✿ body control
- ✿ physical fitness
- ✿ sequencing
- ✿ creative expression

Safety:

✓ Be sure area is clear of objects.

✓ Consider using scarves while standing on a non-skid surface.

How you can help:

✓ Stress accurate, controlled throws.

✓ Emphasize grasping scarf in the middle by pinching it with the thumb and index finger before throwing.

✓ Encourage watching the scarf's movement rather than looking where your hands are.

INSTRUCTION AND MOVEMENT CHALLENGE PACKET
"Make It Take It" ISBN 0-9664413-4-6   © 1999, L. Cox and T. Lubbers
This page is reproducible

Scarves: Movement Challenges

Can you...

✓ place and balance the scarf on your back? On your knee? On what other body parts can you balance the scarf?

✓ wave the scarf high in the air? Close to the floor? At your side? Behind your back?

✓ wave the scarf fast? Slow?

✓ swing the scarf in a big circle over your head? In a small circle at your side?

✓ move the scarf back and forth like a windshield wiper?

✓ draw a figure 8 with your scarf?

✓ sit on the floor and pass the scarf around your body from one hand to the other hand?

✓ place the scarf on your head and walk slowly? What other body parts can you place the scarf on while moving? What other ways can you use to move from place to place (for example: Walk quickly. Walk on your tiptoes. Skip)?

✓ place scarf on your upper chest and run so fast that the scarf stays in place?

✓ place the scarf on the floor and jump over it without touching it?

✓ balance on one foot while waving the scarf over your head?

INSTRUCTION AND MOVEMENT CHALLENGE PACKET
"Make It Take It" ISBN 0-9664413-4-6   © 1999, L. Cox and T. Lubbers

Can you toss a scarf in the air...

- ✓ and see how high you can count before the scarf to touches the floor?

- ✓ and sit down on the floor to catch it?

- ✓ with your right hand and catch it in your right hand?

- ✓ with your right hand and catch it with your left hand?

 ✓ turn around in a circle and catch the scarf before it hits the floor?

 ✓ clap your hands and catch the scarf?

- ✓ catch it below waist height? Below knee height?

- ✓ catch it by reaching under your leg?

- ✓ volley it in the air like a volleyball?

Can you...

- ✓ hold the scarf at two corners, blow on it and keep it up with puffs of air?

- ✓ walk around the house, room, or gym tossing and catching a scarf?

- ✓ crumble scarf up in your hand and throw it high in the air and catch it?

- ✓ toss the scarf up with your hand and catch it on your elbow? Catch it on your head or your knee? What other body parts can you use to catch your scarf?

136

INSTRUCTION AND MOVEMENT CHALLENGE PACKET
"Make It Take It" ISBN 0-9664413-4-6   © 1999, L. Cox and T. Lubbers
This page is reproducible

✓ place the scarf on your elbow, toss it in the air and catch it with your hand? What other body parts can you use to toss your scarf?

✓ place the scarf on your foot, lift your foot to kick it in the air, and catch it in your hand?

With one scarf held in each hand can you...

✓ swing them up and down simultaneously? Move one up in the air while moving the other one down?

✓ hold your arms out to the sides and make big circles?

✓ shake one high in the air and the other low?

✓ shake one in front of your body and the other behind your back?

✓ toss both at the same time, and catch both scarves with the same hand that tossed them?

✓ toss both at the same time, and cross hands (arms) to catch them?

✓ toss them up one at a time and catch them? (toss, toss, catch, catch)

With a friend can you...

✓ sit on the floor and catch a scarf that a friend who is standing up drops?

✓ play the game, **AMIMAL TAIL TAG**? Each person should tuck a corner of a scarf in the back of their clothing (i.e. belt or waistband) for their tail. Try to move quickly and snatch each other's tail.

INSTRUCTION AND MOVEMENT CHALLENGE PACKET
"Make It Take It" ISBN 0-9664413-4-6   © 1999, L. Cox and T. Lubbers

✓ run and catch the scarf that your partner tosses? Have your friend stand about 5 to 10 feet away from you and toss the scarf in the air. Can you run and catch the scarf before it touches the floor?

✓ stand behind your friend and toss and catch the scarves?

✓ stand back to back and toss one or more scarves to each other?

✓ stand face to face with one person holding two scarves and throwing them simultaneously to you?

✓ stand side by side with inside hands joined and throw scarves to each other using your outside hands?

✓ stand face to face while holding a scarf, throw it high in the air and trade places with your friend? Your friend can catch the scarf while moving to the new place.

INSTRUCTION AND MOVEMENT CHALLENGE PACKET
"Make It Take It" ISBN 0-9664413-4-6   © 1999, L. Cox and T. Lubbers

CREATING MOVEMENT WITH STREAMERS AND RIBBON STICKS

A Collection of Movement Challenges

Ribbon sticks or streamers are small enough to carry in a backpack or tote bag and can be readily available for play. They provide a wide range of vigorous or calm creative movement opportunities. These pieces of equipment can be used inside or outside, by oneself or with a friend, and with or without music.

Kit Contents

1. **Container**

   Ziplock™-type bag, cloth bag, or box

2. **Equipment**

   Two or more ribbon sticks and/or streamers

   Recorded music on cassette tape/CD (optional)

3. **Instructions and Movement Challenge Packet**

   Decorative "cover page" (may wish to laminate)

   Instructional pages that explain what children will gain, safety precautions, and hints on how you can help

   Movement challenge pages

Streamer and Ribbon Stick Construction

Durable/reusable ribbon sticks

1. Cut 1/2" or 5/8" dowels, plumbers pipe (PVC pipe) or plastic golf tube into lengths of about 10-12". The length and diameter may vary depending on the age of the child or materials available.

2. Sand ends and glue with hot glue gun a small craft type pom-pom ball on one end for color and as a safety cushion.

3. Cut a ribbon from a piece of fabric (cotton, nylon, solid color, print, or neon colors) about 2" wide and 20" to 36" long. The length of the fabric should vary with the height of the child, i.e. longer ribbons for taller children. Nylon fabric may need the edges seared with a heat source to prevent fraying. Cotton fabric may need the edges cut with a pinking scissors to avoid fraying.

4. Glue the ribbon near the end of stick that has the pom-pom ball attached.

Disposable ribbon sticks

1. Glue, tape, or staple a crepe paper streamer to an empty cardboard paper towel cylinder or rolled newspaper section.

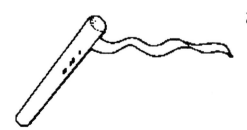

2. The length of the streamer and the colors used may vary.

Streamers (same as above minus the handle)

1.   Cut a 20-36 inch long and a 2 inch wide piece of colorful fabric or a length of crepe paper.

2.   Fastened fabric or crepe paper to a drapery rod ring.

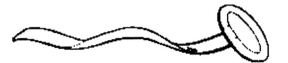

CREATING MOVEMENT WITH STREAMERS AND RIBBON STICKS

A Collection of Movement Challenges

Ribbon sticks or streamers are small enough to carry in a backpack or tote bag and can be readily available for play. They provide a wide range of vigorous or calm creative movement opportunities. These pieces of equipment can be used inside or outside, by oneself or with a friend, and with or without music.

INSTRUCTION AND MOVEMENT CHALLENGE PACKET
"Make It Take It" ISBN 0-9664413-4-6   Copyright 1999, L. Cox and T. Lubbers

Streamers and Ribbon Sticks: Instructions

What children will gain:

- creative expression
- rhythm skills
- locomotor skills
- non-locomotor movements
- visual tracking
- body/space awareness

- midline crossing
- body control
- physical fitness
- sequencing
- cognitive skills
- movement imitation skills

Safety:

✓ Children may need assistance in determining a safe amount of space so that their ribbon stick does not bump another person.

✓ Provide enough empty space for safe locomotor movements (for running, galloping, or skipping) with the ribbon stick or streamer.

✓ Check ends of ribbon sticks periodically to see that the soft pompom ball (padding) is in place and for splinters (if the handle is wooden).

How you can help:

✓ Encourage children to explore movement. Try different ways of moving the ribbon stick/streamer or moving with the ribbon stick. Use questions such as "What other ways can you..."

✓ Encourage control of body and stick/streamer by using questions such as "Can you move without bumping into anyone or anything?"

✓ Encourage children to choose favorite music/songs. You may wish to sing a song together, use a cassette tape/CD, or turn on your favorite radio station.

INSTRUCTION AND MOVEMENT CHALLENGE PACKET
"Make It Take It" ISBN 0-9664413-4-6   © 1999, L. Cox and T. Lubbers

Streamers and Ribbon Sticks: Movement Challenges

Can you move the streamer/ribbon stick (with or without music)...

✓ in the space around your body?

- move it high (How high can you stretch?)
- down low (Can you wiggle it like a snake or worm? Can you sweep the floor with it like a broom?)
- behind your back? At your side? At your other side (cross midline)? Close to your body? Far away from you body?

✓ at different speeds?

- move it fast
- move it slow
- move it at medium speed

✓ in different pathways?

- move it up and down (vertical) or side to side (horizontal)
- move it in a zig-zag, circular or figure 8 path
- move it in a shape/pathway of a number or letter

✓ with different sizes of movement?

- draw a big circle
- make small zig zags

✓ with different kinds of movements such as shaking it, swinging it, or spinning it like a tornado?

Put the streamer/ribbon stick in the other hand and do all of the above activities.

INSTRUCTION AND MOVEMENT CHALLENGE PACKET
"Make It Take It" ISBN 0-9664413-4-6   © 1999, L. Cox and T. Lubbers

With your streamer/ribbon stick, can you combine the elements of space, speed, size, and type of movement by...

- ✓ shaking it at fast (or slow, or medium) speeds while holding it up high (or low)?

- ✓ making fast (or slow), big (or small) circles, in front of your body (or at the side)?

- ✓ moving it on the right (or left) side of your body with fast (or slow) and small (or large) zig zag movements?

- ✓ swinging it fast (or slow) with big (or little) swings?

- ✓ moving it fast (or slow), high in the air (or low) while twisting your body?

With your streamer/ribbon stick can you...

- ✓ create a sequence of movements? (i.e. swing the stick 4 times, then shake it 4 times, then swing it again 4 times) The number and types of movements can be increased to challenge the child's memory.

- ✓ imitate a sequence of movements performed by a friend?

- ✓ create movement patterns that suggest concepts or objects? (i.e. clouds, rain or snow, blowing or falling leaves, water moving or ocean waves, a merry-go-round, or a dancer dancing)

Can you move around the yard, gym, or room (with or without music) by...

- ✓ running while holding the streamer/ribbon stick up high? Down low? Out to the side?

146

"Make It Take It" ISBN 0-9664413-4-6   © 1999, L. Cox and T. Lubbers

✓ galloping and moving the streamer/ribbon stick in a circle?

✓ jumping (or hopping on one foot) and making the streamer/ribbon stick move up on one jump and down on the next jump?

✓ jumping forward and backward while keeping the streamer/ribbon stick moving?

✓ hopping on one foot in a side to side motion while keeping the streamer/ribbon stick moving?

✓ varying the locomotor activity used with the previous challenges? Try sliding, leaping, or skipping.

With you and a friend each holding a streamer/ribbon stick can you...

✓ mirror/imitate each other's movements? Take turns being the leader and try a variety of movements while sitting, standing, or tall kneeling.

✓ walk behind or follow your friend while imitating what the leader does?

- vary with the leader moving in different pathways such as zig zag or circular
- vary with the leader moving in different locomotor patterns such as run, jump, hop, gallop, skip, leap, slide, or skate
- be in a parade and march to some favorite music

INSTRUCTION AND MOVEMENT CHALLENGE PACKET
"Make It Take It" ISBN 0-9664413-4-6   © 1999, L. Cox and T. Lubbers

With a streamer/ribbon stick in <u>each</u> hand, (with or without music), can you...

✓ explore different ways of moving the streamer/ribbon sticks?

  - shake, twist, or swing
  - swing them up and down simultaneously
  - move one up while moving the other down
  - swing them across your body (like giving yourself a hug) and then out to your sides

✓ move each streamer/ribbon stick in a different pathways? Try zig-zags, circles, or straight lines.

✓ imitate or mirror different continuous movements that your friend makes? Take turns being the leader.

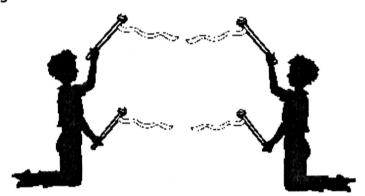

✓ demonstrate a variety of ways to make the streamer/ribbon sticks move at the same time? How many different ways can you think of?

INSTRUCTION AND MOVEMENT CHALLENGE PACKET
"Make It Take It" ISBN 0-9664413-4-6   © 1999, L. Cox and T. Lubbers

INDEX / APPENDIX

Activity Kit / Skill Development Index
(Page 1 of 2)

	Balance	Bilateral Coordination	Body Control	Body/Space Awareness	Cognitive Skills	Creative Expression	Eye-Foot Coordination	Eye-Hand Coordination
Balloons and Balloon Balls	✓	✓	✓	✓				✓
Balls		✓	✓	✓			✓	✓
Beanbags	✓	✓	✓	✓	✓		✓	✓
Bubbles		✓	✓	✓			✓	✓
Fishing	✓		✓	✓	✓			✓
Hoops	✓		✓	✓	✓	✓	✓	✓
Racquets and Bats			✓	✓	✓			✓
Ropes	✓	✓	✓	✓	✓	✓		
Scarves		✓	✓	✓		✓		✓
Streamers & Ribbon Sticks		✓	✓	✓	✓	✓		

Activity Kit / Skill Development Index
(Page 2 of 2)

	Locomotor Skills	Midline Crossing	Non-locomotor skills	Physical Fitness	Rhythm Skills	Sequencing Skills	Visual Tracking
Balloons and Balloon Balls				✓		✓	✓
Balls				✓		✓	✓
Beanbags				✓		✓	✓
Bubbles		✓				✓	✓
Fishing		✓				✓	
Hoops	✓		✓	✓		✓	
Racquets and Bats		✓		✓		✓	✓
Ropes	✓			✓	✓	✓	
Scarves			✓	✓	✓	✓	✓
Streamers & Ribbon Sticks	✓	✓	✓	✓	✓	✓	✓

Group Checkout Form

	Name:	Name:	Name:
	Date Taken / Date Returned	Date Taken / Date Returned	Date Taken / Date Returned
Balloon Ball			
Balls			
Beanbags			
Bubbles			
Fishing			
Hoops			
Racquets & Bats			
Ropes			
Scarves			
Streamers & Ribbon Sticks			

INSTRUCTION AND MOVEMENT CHALLENGE PACKET
"Make It Take It" ISBN 0-9664413-4-6   © 1999, L. Cox and T. Lubbers
This page is reproducible

Individual Checkout Form

NAME: _____

	Date Taken / Date Returned	Date Taken / Date Returned	Date Taken / Date Returned
Balloon Ball			
Balls			
Beanbags			
Bubbles			
Fishing			
Hoops			
Racquets & Bats			
Ropes			
Scarves			
Streamers & Ribbon Sticks			

INSTRUCTION AND MOVEMENT CHALLENGE PACKET
"Make It Take It" ISBN 0-9664413-4-6   © 1999, L. Cox and T. Lubbers
This page is reproducible

Home Activity Feedback Form

Child's Name:

Parent/Caregiver's Name:

Dates Activity was Used:

Name of Activity:

1. What did your child do well?

   _____

   _____

   _____

2. Did you child need help? How?

   _____

   _____

   _____

3. Do you want/need more information? Explain.

   _____

   _____

   _____

4. Other concerns/comments.

   _____

   _____

   _____

INSTRUCTION AND MOVEMENT CHALLENGE PACKET
"Make It Take It" ISBN 0-9664413-4-6   © 1999, L. Cox and T. Lubbers

Sample Activity Station

Permanent poster located near play area

Poster has removable/attachable cards that can be created for different activities

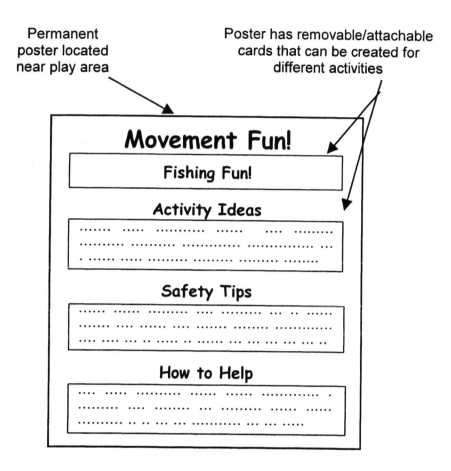

Movement Fun!

Fishing Fun!

Activity Ideas

Safety Tips

How to Help

Position Illustrations

Straddle Sit   Long Sit   Side Sit   Tailor Sit

Kneel   Tall Kneel   Half Kneel   Squat

Wheelbarrow Position   Crab Position

INSTRUCTION AND MOVEMENT CHALLENGE PACKET
"Make It Take It" ISBN 0-9664413-4-6   © 1999, L. Cox and T. Lubbers
This page is reproducible

Fish Patterns

INSTRUCTION AND MOVEMENT CHALLENGE PACKET
"Make It Take It"   ISBN 0-9664413-4-6   © 1999, L. Cox and T. Lubbers

For information about this and other Tekna Books titles, please visit our website.

www.teknabooks.com